Proverbs 31

Living in Godly Wisdom

NAOMI SCHMIDT

More by this author:

Ruth – Living in God's unfailing faithfulness

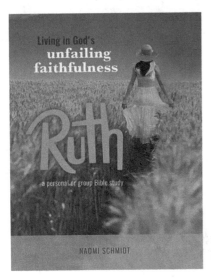

You can see yourself in Ruth, whether you relate to her tainted background, the loss of a loved one, or the feeling that you don't belong. If you have ached for fullness or love, if you have wept or suffered anxiety in waiting, if you have struggled to love someone who is bitter or angry, then you can relate to Ruth. Single? Married? Widowed? She is all those things.

But here's where you will certainly relate to Ruth—you need a Savior.

This beautiful story of redemption is about grace. The grace Ruth received is the same grace we have through faith in Christ—it is the grace we are called to share with others.

Philippians – Living in the joy of Christ

Chained to a Roman guard and facing a death sentence, Paul wrote a letter overflowing with joy. How could Paul remain so joyful in such suffering? We want to know because we want to live in joy like Paul—brimming with grace, love, and a passion for souls. We want our joy to remain melded with Christ, uninhibited by hardships or suffering.

Paul teaches us about joy, unity, humility, and contentedness. He delights in the advancement of the Gospel and the blessing of his ministry companions. He offers powerful warnings and gives godly instruction for Christian living. His dear friends in Philippi teach us about partnership in ministry and commitment to the Gospel. Learn to focus on grace and be filled with joy in all circumstances.

Available at amazon.com or nph.net

Proverbs 31

Living in Godly Wisdom

NAOMI SCHMIDT

Christ in the Word Publishing, 2022

ISBN: 979-8-218-00019-6
Cover Design: Naomi Schmidt/Canva/Getty Images
Edited by Valerie Bodden
"Modest is Hottest" by Dawn Schulz, used with permission

All Scripture quotations, unless otherwise indicated, are taken from the Holy Bible, New International Version®, NIV®. Copyright ©1973, 1978, 1984, 2011 by Biblica, Inc.™ Used by permission of Zondervan. All rights reserved worldwide. www.zondervan.comThe "NIV" and "New International Version" are trademarks registered in the United States Patent and Trademark Office by Biblica, Inc.™

Scripture quotations marked CEB are from the COMMON ENGLISH BIBLE. © Copyright 2011 COMMON ENGLISH BIBLE. All rights reserved. Used by permission. (www.CommonEnglishBible.com).
Scripture quotations marked CEV are from the Contemporary English Version Copyright © 1991, 1992, 1995 by American Bible Society, Used by Permission.
Scripture quotations marked EHV are from the Holy Bible, Evangelical Heritage Version ® (EHV ®) © 2017 Wartburg Project, Inc. All rights reserved. Used by permission.
Scripture quotations marked ESV are from The ESV® Bible (The Holy Bible, English Standard Version®), copyright © 2001 by Crossway, a publishing ministry of Good News Publishers. Used by permission. All rights reserved.
Scripture quotations marked GNT are from the Good News Translation in Today's English Version- Second Edition Copyright © 1992 by American Bible Society. Used by Permission.
All Scripture marked with the designation "GW" is taken from GOD'S WORD®. © 1995, 2003, 2013, 2014, 2019, 2020 by God's Word to the Nations Mission Society. Used by permission.
Scripture quotations marked HCSB are taken from the Holman Christian Standard Bible®, Used by Permission HCSB ©1999,2000,2002,2003,2009 Holman Bible Publishers. Holman Christian Standard Bible®, Holman CSB®, and HCSB® are federally registered trademarks of Holman Bible Publishers.
Scripture quotations marked MSG are taken from THE MESSAGE, copyright © 1993, 2002, 2018 by Eugene H. Peterson. Used by permission of NavPress, represented by Tyndale House Publishers. All rights reserved.
Scripture marked NASB is taken from the NEW AMERICAN STANDARD BIBLE(R), Copyright (C) 1960, 1962, 1963, 1968, 1971, 1972, 1973, 1975, 1977, 1995 by The Lockman Foundation. Used by permission.
Scripture marked NCV is taken from the New Century Version®. Copyright © 2005 by Thomas Nelson. Used by permission. All rights reserved.
Scripture marked NKJV is taken from the New King James Version®. Copyright © 1982 by Thomas Nelson. Used by permission. All rights reserved.
Scripture quotations marked NLT are taken from the Holy Bible, New Living Translation, copyright ©1996, 2004, 2015 by Tyndale House Foundation. Used by permission of Tyndale House Publishers, Carol Stream, Illinois 60188. All rights reserved.
Scripture quotations marked NLT are taken from the Holy Bible, New Living Translation, copyright © 1996, 2004, 2007 by Tyndale House Foundation. Used by permission of Tyndale House Publishers, Inc., Carol Stream, IL 60188. All rights reserved.

First printing, Second printing, 2022

How to use this Bible study

5 Topical Lessons

The five lessons in this study are topical. The first lesson is an introduction, but the remaining lessons are grouped thematically. Rather than study the verses individually or numerically, they are arranged to emphasize key characteristics of the Proverbs 31 woman.

Open each lesson by reading Proverbs 31:10-31, then work through the narrative sections. You can read or summarize the paragraphs, or have the participants read them aloud. Read the Scripture verses in each lesson, noting the differences in the various translations that are printed.

Questions and Answer Helps

Many questions in the study are intended to generate personal reflection and group discussion. Give the participants time to think about their answers.

There are answer helps in the back of the book if you want to make sure you're on track. Some questions have specific answers, while others have answers that will vary.

Applications

Participants are encouraged to apply the principles of the text to their personal life. It is important for women to share their experiences or insights and ask questions.
There will also be time to apply these truths to the church as the Bride of Christ.

Translations

Quite a few translations of Proverbs 31:10-31 are printed in the middle of the book.
At the beginning of each lesson, read a different translation to remember the big picture. The translations are also good for personal reading and meditation. You'll be amazed at how many unique words will jump out or give you a new insight as you are reading.

Journal of Personal Reflections

The author's journal of personal reflections takes each verse in the chapter as a thought for meditation. The journal is most suitable for reading at a time other than Bible study because the thoughts don't specifically support the learning objectives for each lesson. It will also work well for personal devotions.

Reproducible Study Guides

Reproducible study guides are available online at christintheword.wordpress.com.
The questions from each lesson and brief summaries are included to help participants follow the development of each section.

Check out all the resources at christintheword.wordpress.com

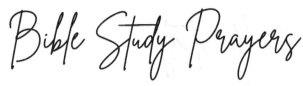

Bible Study Prayers

These opening prayers can be read by an individual or the group to further engage the participants. Closing prayers are printed at the end of each lesson for similar use.

1. Heavenly Father, as we gather together to study your Word, we pray that you would send your Holy Spirit to be with us. Clear our minds from the distractions and concerns of the day and open our hearts to receive the truth of your Word. Guide our study and discussions that we may grow closer to you in all we do and say. Strengthen our faith according to the promises in your Word and bind our hearts to one another in fellowship and love. May the words of our mouths and the meditation of our hearts be pleasing in your sight, O Lord, our Rock and Redeemer, Amen.

2. Lord Jesus, as we gather around your Word, we pray that you would teach us as children learning from their dear Father. Remind us of the blessed waters of baptism that washed us clean and filled us with your Spirit. Give us faith to be child-like in accepting your truth with unquestioning hearts; but grow us into mature believers who love your Word and search its depths for your wisdom and love. Guide and direct our study that we may keep your truth pure and grow in the knowledge and grace of your Son, in whose name we pray. Amen.

3. Lord Jesus, it is a privilege and pleasure to gather together as sisters in Christ to study your Word. Bless our time together and strengthen our faith with your Word. Deepen our understanding of your truths and grant us wisdom as we learn to apply all that we have studied. When we see the truth of the law in your Word, pierce our hearts to see our sin, and then quickly comfort us with the blessing of your gospel. When we feel discouraged because we cannot keep all your commands, remind us that Christ has indeed lived a perfect life on our behalf. Help us focus on your amazing gifts of grace, forgiveness, and righteousness. May our time together leave us with joyful hearts, renewed faith, confidence in the gospel, and motivation to live for your glory. In the name of Jesus our Savior we pray. Amen.

4. Lord Jesus, in your grace and love, you have given us your Word as a light for our path to guide us in our journey of life. But your Word gives us more than just direction; it gives us life itself. Your Word is the power and strength of the church on earth, and it is ours as well. Thank you for this priceless gift; lead us to treasure it above all things. Make us diligent students and eager learners that we may grow in grace and wisdom. Open our hearts to understand your teachings that we may be equipped and motivated to faithfully serve you with our gifts by the power of your almighty Word. Bless our study so that all we say and learn is in keeping with your truth; let our hearts and words bring you glory and build our fellowship. In Jesus' name, Amen.

5. O Spirit of God, we come to you, eager to hear your Word with its deep wisdom and flawless truth. We pray that you would strengthen our faith and refine our understanding of Scripture. Give us insights that reflect what you want us to know and advance our thinking through the clarity of your Word. We listen with trusting hearts, knowing that your Word is holy, inspired, and powerful. We listen in humility, knowing your mercy and forgiveness are undeserved. We listen with hope because you have made us your children through grace. Speak to us now as we gather around your Word to study, meditate, and hear your voice. Lord, be glorified as you make yourself known. Amen.

Dedication

To Jesus,
who continues to speak through the Word.

May your name be praised.

Proverbs 31

LIVING IN GODLY WISDOM

Meet the Woman — Her Introduction — 3

Proverbs 31:1-9
Scripture Snapshots: Esther, Abigail
Living in Godly Wisdom: As I See Myself
Living in Godly Wisdom: As the Church Shows Our Need

Look in the Mirror — Her Image — 11

Proverbs 31:10, 11, 12, 29, 30
Scripture Snapshots: Eve, Mary Magdalene
Living in Godly Wisdom: As I Bear God's Image
Living in Godly Wisdom: As the Church Reflects God's Image

Delight in Her Love — Her Relationships — 19

Proverbs 31:23, 25, 26, 28, 31
Scripture Snapshots: Naomi, Mary the mother of Jesus
Living in Godly Wisdom: As I Influence Others in My Relationships
Living in Godly Wisdom: As the Church Builds Relationships

Watch Her Serve — Her Tasks — 27

Proverbs 31:13, 15, 17, 19, 20, 22
Scripture Snapshots: Ruth, Dorcas
Living in Godly Wisdom: As I Serve Others
Living in Godly Wisdom: As the Church Serves in Ministry

Follow Her Lead — Her Opportunities — 35

Proverbs 31:14, 16, 18, 21, 24, 27
Scripture Snapshots: Deborah, Lydia
Living in Godly Wisdom: As I Accept Leadership
Living in Godly Wisdom: As the Church Offers Leadership

Further Blessings

Proverbs 31 –
Various translations are quoted in this study.
You can read Proverbs 31:10-31 in each of these translations here:

Common English Bible (CEB)	44
Contemporary English Version (CEV)	46
Evangelical Heritage Version (EHV)	48
English Standard Version (ESV)	50
Good News Translation (GNT)	52
God's WORD Translation (GW)	53
Holman Christian Standard Bible (HCSB)	55
The Message (MSG)	57
New American Standard Bible (NASB)	59
New Century Version (NCV)	61
New International Version (NIV)	63
New King James Version (NKJV)	65
New Living Translation (NLT)	67
New Life Version (NLV)	69

A Journal of Personal Reflections	71
Proverbs 31 Applications and Attitudes	92
Answer Helps	93

Study Objectives

- Learn the setting and purpose of the wisdom in Proverbs 31.
- Hear God's commands and remember your need for a Savior.
- Learn to love the design described and personified in Proverbs 31.
- Live knowing Christ's righteousness is God's gift to you.
- Examine situations in Scripture where women reflect God's image.
- Base your value and self-worth on what God says is true.
- Influence and encourage others whom God has put on your path.
- Be energized by the Gospel to serve others.
- Gain wisdom to offer Christ-like leadership.

LIVING IN GODLY WISDOM

Preface

Discouragement, with a tinge of resentment. That's how I think most women view the woman in Proverbs 31. Why wouldn't we feel that way? Here is a woman who gets up before dawn, takes care of her family, helps people in need, manages a profitable business, and works late into the night.

We don't need a reminder of all the things we could be doing. We already know what it is to be overwhelmed.

What we really need is wisdom to manage it all.

But Proverbs 31 gives us so much more than just wisdom. It begins by tugging at our hearts with an honest assessment of where we stand before God. It strips us of self-reliance. It reveals our sin with painful clarity because we are not by nature the women God designed us to be. It doesn't say, "Try harder." Instead, the Word offers wisdom beautifully sheathed in grace. It points to the grace of God and enables us to respond with humble gratitude. Forgiven, we joyfully ask, "How can I show you my love and thankfulness? Teach me to make godly decisions in my life!"

Proverbs 31 gives us wisdom as we seek those holy desires.

This entire chapter is like a scrapbook of wisdom. Like slowly turning pages, each verse shapes our thinking with snapshots of a woman's relationships and opportunities. As we read about those she helped, we see how God works through us in daily living. As we reflect on her skills and energy, we remember God also gives us abilities and strength. As we linger on this woman's days of grace, we gain mature insights about ourselves. We meditate on her activity and find godly priorities for our abundant life.

Verse after verse, we see glimpses of God working through this woman's life. Her character, family, relationships, and work all reflect God's grace and love. We recognize the truth that God calls and equips each of us to flourish in every aspect of our lives as believers. We become confident that Christ's work of salvation makes daily tasks into *"living sacrifices, holy and pleasing to God"* (Romans 12:1).

Preface

These are not commands you must carry out or instructions on how to be a *really* good woman. The point isn't, "Do all this stuff, and you'll be loved—or happy." It isn't even saying, "If you *really* loved God, you would . . ." Instead, these are God's loving words to guide and strengthen you. This woman's entire life is captured with beauty and joy. And it blushes with wisdom.

This study of Proverbs 31 presents five key points:
- Hear God's truth about sin.
- Learn what it means to bear God's image.
- Value relationships from God's perspective.
- See a godly purpose in your tasks.
- Offer Christ-like, servant leadership to others.

Application to the Church

The Bride of Christ is the church. As we look at the beautiful Christian woman in Proverbs 31, we see hints of God's holy church. With more than just guidance for wise living, she gives us an uplifting perspective of Christ's beloved Bride, the church.

CHURCH

The word "church" can be used many ways.

In this study, it will refer to all people everywhere who believe in Jesus as their Savior. Only God can see faith in hearts, but there is one body, joined together by faith in Christ. This body of believers is the church. It is also called the Bride of Christ.

We see this wondrous mystery described in Ephesians 5:31-32, *"For this reason a man will leave his father and mother and be united to his wife, and the two will become one flesh.* [32] *This is a profound mystery—but I am talking about Christ and the church."*

Each lesson in this study takes time to consider how the church parallels the description of this godly woman. Like this woman, the church is filled with the image of God, loving relationships, active service, and leadership that reflects Christ. God's plan of salvation through Christ is the foundation and motivation for hope, life, and service.

It blesses us to see how God's design is clearly woven into the fabric of our lives, both individually and collectively—as His Bride, the church. The Proverbs 31 woman reflects the Lord in many ways. The church reflects Him with even greater glory. As you study the Proverbs 31 woman, keep the Bride of Christ in mind. Reflect on the similarities and let them deepen your love and appreciation for God's gift of the church.

Proverbs 31

LIVING IN GODLY WISDOM: LESSON ONE

Meet the Woman — Her Introduction

Proverbs 31 was written during a peaceful, prosperous time in Israel's history. God's people were enjoying the wisdom of Solomon, the music of the Psalms, and the world-renowned beauty of God's temple in Jerusalem. Here is a basic timeline of Old Testament history.

The divine advice laid out in Proverbs came just after King David's reign, when his son, Solomon, had taken the throne. Israel was a powerful nation, and Solomon had secured many alliances with political marriages. But with more than 700 wives and 300 concubines, Solomon was a deplorable example of how to treasure God's gift of women and marriage. Solomon was wise, but he was far from perfect.

Yet during this time, God crafted the compelling description of a godly woman and unveiled everything that is good as He portrayed her life.

This holy wisdom still speaks to us nearly 3,000 years later. Though the world around us is dramatically different, time hasn't changed the value, description, or truth about godly women. But these verses don't speak only to women. This chapter teaches men to cherish godly women and remember their value. Proverbs 31 tells men about the many and varied gifts of Christian women—and the God-pleasing way to treat them.

This chapter helps women grasp the fullness and beauty of living for Christ. It affirms how much their gifts are needed and the blessing they are to others. It paints a beautiful picture of the various partnerships God has given for women to express His love.

Meet the Woman – Her Introduction

The depth and breadth of this holy description will refresh your faith and deepen your appreciation for women in every setting of life. Instead of begrudging the Proverbs 31 woman, you will enjoy the opportunity to meet her.

The entire book of Proverbs teaches wisdom, godly values, and honest consequences. But chapter 31 includes the only advice written by the obscure "King Lemuel," who received wise counsel from his mother. The chapter begins with an "oracle" (teaching) that warns against the temptations of wine and women. Lemuel's mother taught him not to waste his gifts or misuse his authority.

Listen to her warning.

Proverbs 31:1-9 (EHV)

The words of Lemuel, a king.
An oracle that his mother used, to teach him discipline:
² *What are you doing, my son!*
What are you doing, son from my womb!
What are you doing, son of my vows!
³ *Do not give your strength to women.*
Do not give your ways to those who destroy kings.
⁴ *It is not for kings, Lemuel,*
it is not for kings to drink wine,
nor for rulers to crave beer.
⁵ *If he does, he will drink and forget what is decreed.*
He will change the legal rights of all the oppressed.
⁶ *Give beer to someone who is perishing*
and wine to one whose soul is bitter.
⁷ *He will drink and forget his poverty,*
and he will no longer remember his trouble.
⁸ *Speak up for those who cannot speak.*
Speak for the rights of all those who are defenseless.
⁹ *Speak up, judge fairly,*
and defend the oppressed and needy.

The opening verses of this chapter are rather striking and ugly.

You may be tempted to skip over this section and start at verse ten with a clean, fresh sheet of paper. You may just want to begin with the lovely picture of a woman who is redeemed by Christ and filled with His Spirit. But don't.

Meet the Woman – Her Introduction

Before you meet the woman God esteems and values, He begins by reminding you of the decaying, evil nature of sin that destroys faith, corrupts lives, and undermines society. Before you hear about the beauty of godly women, you see the sinful, selfish state of all humanity. God calls out the degrading transgressions of sexual sin, addiction, and injustice. He announces their vulgar nature and consequences. He reminds you that sin is an offense to Him.

Your own conscience has heard King Lemuel's mother as she gasps, *"What are you doing?"* And who of us has not needed to hear that voice?

The Word points out our sin—and we need to remember that we are sinners! But the Word also reveals God's plan of salvation in Christ, our Savior. His plan gives us undeserved love and renewed hope. As our faith grows, we long for a deeper knowledge and understanding of God—and He instructs us through the Word. You can hear Him teaching in Proverbs 31, rebuking and correcting us. God gives guidance for life in a godless world and encouragement to flourish in Christian love. All this wisdom is surrounded by grace that frees us to respond.

1. In a chapter that portrays the beauty and value of Christian women, why do the opening verses have a masculine tone?

2. What ungodly influences or examples heighten the importance of sharing this godly advice and encouragement with both young men and young women?

3. Where can you offer godly wisdom like Lemuel's mother, and where could you be more intentional as a Christian influence?

Meet the Woman – Her Introduction

Scripture Snapshots — Esther and Abigail

If you search the Scriptures to find out whether a godly woman has ever lived with a man who meets the description in Proverbs 31:1-9, you will find several.

Consider the Persian Queen Esther.

King Xerxes reigned 500 years after Solomon, when the Persian Empire was losing the battle for world dominance. Xerxes was proud, wealthy, and crazed with a hunger for power—and his palace was tarnished by pride, envy, and drunkenness. Xerxes' commander, Haman, was also jealous for honor—and nursed a bitter hatred for the Jews. He convinced King Xerxes to sign a decree that would slaughter God's chosen people. The annihilation was planned and the date was chosen. The Jews had one year to live.

ESTHER

Esther did not tell the King she was a Jew or that her Hebrew name was Hadassah. The victory of the Jews over Persian forces is still celebrated today—it is the Festival of Purim.

But a Jewish orphan named Esther was queen of Persia. She was selected from a harem of beautiful women gathered from every province in the king's realm. Who but God could have granted her a royal position for such a time as this? When Esther learned of Haman's evil plot to attack the Jews, she was afraid to approach the king. Even as queen, she faced the possibility of execution for approaching Xerxes without being summoned by him. She fasted and prayed for three days. Torn between faith and fear, she went to plead for her people. The king granted her an appearance and responded to her plea. The Jews were saved despite Xerxes' wild temper and Haman's hateful plan.

The evil actions of others may draw you into your worst nightmare. But God's strength is with you even when you feel weak and overwhelmed.

4. Identify verses in the book of Esther that highlight her difficult situation.

Meet the Woman – Her Introduction

You should also know the story of Abigail in 1 Samuel 25.

Abigail was a beautiful and intelligent woman married to a brute named Nabal (**nay**-bull). Her story begins during sheep shearing season, a joyous time of work marked by celebration and thankfulness.

David and his men had been living in the wilderness near Carmel and protected Nabal's sheep from wild animals and perilous threats. David sent ten young men to Nabal to request food for his army during the festivities, but Nabal refused the request and mocked David. When David received Nabal's insulting response, he gathered 400 of his mighty men to wipe out Nabal's estate—and Nabal got drunk.

ABIGAIL

After Nabal's death, Abigail married King David, settled in Hebron, and bore his second son, Daniel. There is no further mention of this son.

With wisdom and grace, Abigail quickly gathered an extravagant amount of food and met David as he descended the hillside in a rage. She approached the anointed king with respect and humility, mindful of God's high calling to this shepherd boy from Bethlehem. She spoke to David about his godly reputation and dissuaded him from his murderous and vengeful plan. Her quick actions and gentle spirit saved Nabal's defenseless household and preserved David's reputation as God's loyal servant.

In this traumatic moment of darkness, Abigail's words and actions gave evidence of God's power and strength. She serves as a shining example of how God uses believers even when evil rears its ugly head. Satan had a plan to hurt innocent people, exalt a brutal fool, and mar the reputation of God's chosen king. But God's grace and power were victorious.

5. How do the accounts of Esther and Abigail help when your life as a Christian is hard, dark, frightening, or traumatic?

Meet the Woman – Her Introduction

Living in Godly Wisdom — As I See Myself

Proverbs 31 begins with a mother's clear warning against evil with examples of sin's destruction that are too familiar to us. The opening verses remind us that God has a perfect standard of justice—and humanity fails to keep it. Sadly, not much has changed over thousands of years.

As you learn about being a godly woman, start by remembering your own battle against sin and be braced for a difficult life in a sinful world. Satan unleashes cruel and devastating schemes—and sometimes Christian living feels impossible as we face the devil, the world, and our own sinful flesh.

You saw the trials of Esther and Abigail, and though your hardships aren't anything like those situations, you will struggle. It may be a relationship that drains your heart and withers your strength. It may be a battle with something overwhelming, unfair, or hopeless. You may need courage to do what is right.

> **TIM KELLER**
>
> *It is not the strength of your faith but the object of your faith that actually saves you.*

God wants you to know about Esther and Abigail because He wants you to know about Him. God isn't showing you these women to say, "See how strong you can be!" God wants you to see how strong He is. Don't look at the strength of their faith—look at the strength of their God. He gives you His strength through Christ.

6. How does the harsh truth about sin prepare and equip you to learn about living as a godly woman?

7. How does the truth about Christ's completed work of redemption prepare and equip you to learn about living as a godly woman?

Living in Godly Wisdom — As the Church Shows Our Need

The church, like King Lemuel's wise mother, knows the evil nature and hateful tyranny of sin. It announces God's eternal judgment and pulls back the curtain to affirm earth's ongoing agony. Like the grim but important introduction, the church proclaims the law to show people the consequences of sin and their need for a Savior. While the world crumbles under the weight of sin and blindly searches to find solutions, the church knows exactly what the problem is: sin. The church calls out sin in a society that barely recognizes its existence.

The evidence of sin is rampant, and the world is overrun with evil. The truth of God has been exchanged for a lie and people decide for themselves what is right. Since the moment sin entered the world, it has continued to rage with hatred and destruction. Believers like Esther and Abigail continue to live in a world that resists God and resents Christianity.

But God's church has faced threats far greater than the aggression of Xerxes or the pride of Nabal. Even the wickedness that surrounds the 21st-century church pales in comparison to Satan, the Prince of Darkness, who attacks the Bride of Christ with legions of demons, strategic precision, and impeccable timing.

But the church prevails in the triumph of Christ's victory over sin, death, and Satan. Jesus promises *"the gates of hell will not overpower it"* (Matthew 16:18, EHV).

The church stands strong as a beacon of light, called by God to proclaim Christ, make disciples, and strengthen believers through the Word and sacraments.

The church prevails as it clearly proclaims the warning of Proverbs 31: beware of sin, see its consequences, and know there will be a day of judgment.

The church thrives as it boldly declares the one true God glorified in Proverbs 31: He is the faithful Lord who has completed His plan of salvation. His free gifts of grace, forgiveness, and eternal life are for everyone.

Very simply, the church has a call to proclaim repentance and salvation.

God's church—centered in Christ as it teaches sin and grace.

Meet the Woman – Her Introduction

Lord Jesus,

I pray that you would open my heart and teach me the truth of your Word. Help me put aside all my excuses and blindness to sin as I repent and turn to you for forgiveness. Fill me with your grace and strengthen me to live in your righteousness. Let your holy love move me to learn, treasure, and obey your commands. Use your Word to shape my thoughts, desires, and actions every moment. Guide me with your wisdom and lead me with your Spirit. In this dark and faltering world, use me as a voice of truth and a vessel of love. Help me overcome my fears in times of hardship or trials and remind me to trust in you above all things. May all this be done for your glory and the good of your Kingdom that others may learn of your great mercy and unfailing faithfulness. **Amen.**

Things to Remember and Pray About:

Proverbs 31

LIVING IN GODLY WISDOM: LESSON TWO

Look in the Mirror — Her Image

Women have an internal button marked, "You are worthless," and it gets pushed way too often. A thousand things set it off—failure in the face of unrealistic or unreached expectations, the disappointment or disapproval of others, feeling unloved, unappreciated, or overwhelmed because life can be *so* very hard. Sometimes all it takes is a look in a mirror.

But in Proverbs 31, God boldly proclaims what makes a woman beautiful. He announces her priceless value for all to treasure. Her worth—*your* worth—is greater than rubies or jewels. You are worth the blood of Jesus Christ, shed on the cross to make you His own. Christ gave His life for you.

As a new creation in Christ, your renewed identity reflects the image of God, and through Proverbs 31, God wants to enrich your understanding of His image. In this chapter, God fleshes out the fullness, depth, and Spirit of *"a woman who fears the Lord"* (verse 30). Scripture shows this Christian woman reflecting God's holy image in daily living. Her identity reflects God's holiness—her actions reflect His love. Her words are His truth, and His Spirit bears fruits of faith in her life.

Though you may see a title for this section like "The Wife of Noble Character," the truths of this chapter are for you even if you are not married—or your faith is not shared by those you love. This wisdom is not meant only for married women or wives in strong Christian homes. It recognizes and upholds the value, character, and identity of godly women everywhere.

Everyone can learn from these timeless words.

Look in the Mirror – Her Image

A variety of translations are printed here to capture the rich portrayal and central truths about this woman as she bears the image of God.

Proverbs 31:10

- *A wife of noble character who can find? She is worth far more than rubies. (NIV)*
- *Who can find a wife with a strong character? She is worth far more than jewels. (GW)*
- *It is hard to find a good wife, because she is worth more than rubies. (NCV)*

Proverbs 31:25

- *She is clothed with strength and dignity; she can laugh at the days to come. (NIV)*
- *She dresses with strength and nobility, and she smiles at the future. (GW)*
- *She is strong and is respected by the people. She looks forward to the future with joy. (NCV)*

Proverbs 31:30

- *Charm is deceptive, and beauty evaporates, but a woman who has the fear of the Lord should be praised. (GW)*
- *Pleasing ways lie and beauty comes to nothing, but a woman who fears the Lord will be praised. (NLV)*
- *Charm is deceitful, and beauty is vain, but a woman who fears the Lord is to be praised. (ESV)*

Text Notes:

The word *"noble"* in verse 10 of the NIV captures the idea of strength and dignity—other translations call her excellent, worthy, competent, capable, good, truly good, and virtuous. Don't think of this like the nobility of a royal family.

The Proverbs 31 woman is filled with strength and dignity, but she isn't prideful. She draws the love, respect, and admiration of others. Her optimistic joy springs from her faith in God—the unfailing, faithful Lord who saves His people.

She is truly beautiful because God loves her and has designed her to be a vessel of grace and truth. This woman's value and identity are in Christ, and everything good that radiates from her life reflects God's image.

What do these verses help us understand about God? We learn that the Lord is excellent and noble. He is trustworthy and faithful. The Lord Almighty is a helper to the undeserving, and His strength never fails—He never does evil. His strength and dignity are unsurpassed. This is a glimpse of God's holy image and a clear picture of how it is revealed in the lives of believers.

This description isn't God's expectation of you; it is His gift to you. God gives believers His image—He gives you a new identity in Christ.

1. Describe ways you have seen glimpses of God's image in other godly women.

2. What can women do to encourage one another to live as a new creation in Christ?

3. What will change the most as your self-image is realigned with the image of God that has been given to you?

Look in the Mirror – Her Image

Scripture Snapshots — Eve and Mary Magdalene

In Scripture's account of creation, we see how God gave His image to Adam and Eve. God declared that everything was *"very good"* (Genesis 1:31), and awe of God prevailed as man and woman walked with Him in perfect harmony.

This perfect fellowship lasted for a time. But sin soon entered the world, and God's image in humanity was shattered. Sin separated humanity from God, and the offense of sin required a payment. Now the world would know death.

God sent His Son to pay the debt of all sin, and Christ won the victory over death for all people.

God continues to forgive sin, create faith, and restore His image in believers because of Christ.

EVE

God's image given to Eve unveils a relationship wherein Eve wanted what God wanted and loved what God loved.

God's image shines in His children as they are strengthened by the Word and sacraments. God's thoughts, desires, and love are evident as believers reflect the character of their Creator.

We want to know what it looks like to reflect God's image in *our* daily living, but the glimpses from the Garden of Eden don't tell us much. We know God fashioned the perfect woman at creation and then thousands of years later described a noble woman in Proverbs 31. Are there similarities we can learn from? Yes.

Both Eve and the Proverbs 31 woman loved God. They also loved their husbands, had a holy purpose, and served others to share God's love. Each woman reflected God's image and glorified Him in daily living. Both were approved by God. In both texts, man and woman valued each other and were delighted with their Christian partnership. They experienced joy, strength, dignity, and confidence in the future.

Proverbs 31 witnesses to the beautiful design given by God in the Garden of Eden.

4. Compare these verses from Proverbs with Genesis chapters 1-2 and note any similarities.

Mary Magdalene is another beautiful example of God's image reflected in the life of a woman.

Before Mary met Jesus, she was possessed by seven demons who tormented her—we cannot imagine how she suffered. But in His great mercy, Jesus cast out her demons with divine power and authority. He forgave her sins and filled her with His Spirit. Like the Proverbs 31 woman, Mary received grace, holiness, worth, and the identity of Christ. Changed on the inside, her life gave evidence to God's amazing grace and the divine image He had renewed in her.

MARY MAGDALENE

Freed from her demons, Mary was renewed with God's image and her life changed dramatically. She followed and served Christ in His earthly ministry with faithful love and holy living.

Mary's story is important because Satan wants you to feel trapped in sin and condemnation. Satan wants you to think about what you are without Christ and feel the shame of guilt. But through Mary's life, God shows you what it is to be a new creation in Christ, forgiven and free. Mary shows us a life of thankfulness that trusts God's grace. She is no longer ruled by the law of sin and death. Her sins are forgiven, and God's image shines with fruits of faith.

What does the Proverbs 31 woman have in common with Mary Magdalene? Redemption. Humility. Responses of faith that show a willingness to serve others. Joy in being helpful. Fruits of faith that draw attention to the goodness of God and a heart that looks to the good of others. Mary, like the Proverbs 31 woman, took care of others with many acts of service that reflected God's image as a helper.

5. God reveals Himself as a helper, *"Indeed, God is my helper"* (Psalm 54:4, EHV). Since we bear His image, we will also be helpers. Review the life and actions of Mary Magdalene (see page 95 for a complete list of passages). How does her life reflect and give evidence of the truth that God is a helper?

Look in the Mirror – Her Image

Living in Godly Wisdom — As I Bear God's Image

"Who can find a wife of noble character?"

This question isn't just for a man seeking a wife.

Godly men seek the insights and perspectives of their Christian sisters. Women often see things differently, and men know a woman's thoughts are a valuable contribution to the body of Christ. Believers understand the beauty of God's design for partnership—and have a high regard for one another. We look to build one another up.

C. S. LEWIS

A woman's heart should be so close to God that a man should have to chase Him to find her.

Who else is looking for a woman with strong faith?

Young women who want to be mentored, many who long to be encouraged in their faith, and countless women who need help navigating life. Others ache for words of comfort from women who have been comforted by Christ.

Isn't that why you're reading Proverbs 31—because you want to *be* a woman of strong faith? But being a noble woman isn't about your actions. God doesn't look for women with strong faith. He creates them. God gives His image to believers and nurtures their faith through the Word and His Supper.

Clearly, Scripture also describes the sharp contrast of ungodly women. 2 Timothy 3:6 says, *"weak-willed women . . . are loaded down with sins and are swayed by all kinds of evil desires."* Solomon says, *"Her speech is smoother than oil; but in the end she is bitter as gall. . . . She gives no thought to the way of life; her paths are crooked"* (Proverbs 6:3, 4, 6). This description still applies today, and its ugliness compels us to see the importance of our witness. We need to live our faith openly and demonstrate how God intended men and women to live together in love.

6. How do godly men demonstrate that they value godly women?

7. How does your view of ungodly women help or hinder your outreach?

Living in Godly Wisdom — As the Church Reflects God's Image

How is the church like the Proverbs 31 woman? It bears the image of God.

God Himself is revealed as the church preaches the Word and celebrates the sacraments. God gives strength, dignity, hope, and confidence to the church through the completed work of salvation in Christ. Like the woman in Proverbs 31, it is not the outside or visible structure that gives the church value but rather the truth that God dwells in His Temple.

And who is looking for this Holy Bride of Christ?

People looking for relationships and belonging. People who need hope or help in hardship. The weary, broken, and disheartened, but especially those living under the heavy yoke of sin and guilt. Many don't even know what they need or where to look. You can be God's voice saying, "Come and see!"

What do people find in the arms of this Bride? Grace—a treasure worth more than rubies! Jesus called it the *"pearl of great price"* (Matthew 13:46, KJV).

Christians show the church honor and respect—they know it is where God meets His people in the Word. God creates faith in Baptism and strengthens believers through His body and blood. What God gives and institutes, He protects and rules. She belongs to Him, and the Lord will not let her perish.

The image of God is evident in the church as it teaches the pure and holy Word of God. When the church faithfully teaches the truth of Scripture, God's people will see His image more clearly. The church will abound in love, showing mercy to all in need. She will demonstrate the love of Christ with living sacrifices focused on the eternal good of others. She will be marked by compassion, grace, and the fruit of the Spirit. The church will dwell on things that are important to God and embrace His priorities and values. She will love what God loves and will resist the things that God calls evil.

Look for God's image in His Bride, the church.

She reveals God through the truth of Scripture.

Look in the Mirror – Her Image

Creator God,

You have designed me according to your perfect plan, washed me with your grace, and filled me with your love. You dwell within me—what joy is mine! My heart can barely whisper the awe of my soul, but your Word has said it clearly: I bear your image. Oh, Lord strengthen your Spirit in me! Let me reflect your image as I love what you love. Shine through me as I show your mercy and compassion to others. Speak through me as I share your truth unhindered by fear. But when I fail and am tripped up by sin and guilt, turn my eyes to your face and favor. Remind me every morning of your forgiveness and cleansing love, for you are my precious Savior. Tell me again and again to find my priceless value and unchanging worth in you. Refresh and refine me with your love and truth so that I may be a radiant reflection of your holy love. **Amen.**

Things to Remember and Pray About:

Proverbs 31

LIVING IN GODLY WISDOM: LESSON THREE

Delight in Her Love — Her Relationships

We are captivated by the warmth of loving relationships—and the Proverbs 31 woman is a beautiful example for us. Her life is filled with relationships that express God's grace, truth, and hope. The ever-widening scope of her influence begins at home and extends to countless other relationships that are rich with self-sacrificing love and blessed with the admiration of others.

For all the amazing qualities and remarkable skills that she displays, this is likely the blessing that tugs most at our hearts. Her ability to build successful relationships seems so natural. Her husband and children speak well of her, others seek her wisdom, and everyone responds with appreciation.

We pray for something even remotely close to this.

But don't assume that every relationship in her life—or yours—can be so perfect. We live in a broken world. Rather, learn from Scripture how to be a loving, wise, and godly influence in the relationships you have been given. Follow God's wisdom as you build or even struggle in relationships. Be confident that God is working through you far more than what you can see. He often nurtures faith in quiet stillness—He works in moments you never see.

These verses are not a picture of how relationships always work, but they give an example of how God's image is reflected through Christians in their relationships. The Proverbs 31 woman grasps God's intentional plan for her life and is moved by grace to love others in her home, church, and community.

Delight in Her Love – Her Relationships

These verses highlight the relationships of the Proverbs 31 woman. They are arranged in this specific order to reflect her rippling impact.

Proverbs 31:11

- *The heart of her husband safely trusts in her, so he shall have no lack of gain. (NKJV)*
- *Her husband trusts her with all his heart, and he does not lack anything good. (GW)*
- *Her husband can trust her, and she will greatly enrich his life. (NLT)*

Proverbs 31:12

- *She helps him and never harms him all the days of her life. (GW)*
- *She rewards him with good, not evil, all the days of her life. (HCSB)*
- *She does him good and not evil all the days of her life. (NASB)*

Proverbs 31:28

- *Her children show their appreciation, and her husband praises her. (GNT)*
- *Her children praise her,*
  and with great pride her husband says . . . (CEV)
- *Her children and her husband stand up and bless her. In addition, he sings her praises by saying . . . (GW)*

Proverbs 31:23

- *Her husband is respected at the city gate, where he takes his seat among the elders of the land. (NIV)*
- *Her husband is a well-known and respected leader in the city. (CEV)*
- *Her husband is known at the city meetings,*
  where he makes decisions as one of the leaders of the land. (NCV)

Proverbs 31:26

- *She opens her mouth with wisdom and loving instruction is on her tongue. (HCSB)*
- *She opens her mouth with wisdom,*
  And on her tongue is the law of kindness. (NKJV)
- *She opens her mouth in wisdom, and the teaching of kindness is on her tongue. (NASB)*

Text Notes:

The first trait we see in these verses is trust. The Proverbs 31 woman's words and actions bring security to her husband—you can see tenderness and transparency in their relationship. Her husband trusts her to be faithful and is strengthened by her respect. People thrive in a place of trust, safety, and respect. Work to build these valuable attributes into your relationships.

This woman is a helper who serves others to express God's love, starting in her own home. Her words and actions seek the good of others to bless them and never bring harm. She does this every day of her life. (You are probably feeling a pang of guilt right now, but you are also learning—so hear the guidance.)

The husband who loves and appreciates his wife is also respected at the city gate in the business world. We see a marriage where each spouse is invested and delighted in the success of the other. They work for the good of the other and want each other to be blessed.

The children actively express love and appreciation for their mother. Like their father, they speak with kindness and demonstrate love with action.

But this woman is also influential outside the home. She touches neighbors, church friends, extended family, and community members. Her words and actions are wise, loving, and kind. Her nurturing spirit offers instruction and good counsel. She works to build godly relationships wherever God has placed her.

1. What advice would you give a young woman who is seeking to live in loving, Christ-centered relationships?

2. Describe actions that build trust and demonstrate commitment when struggling in a friendship.

3. List three people outside your family who might be influenced by you.

Scripture Snapshots — Naomi and Mary the mother of Jesus

Naomi is an exceptional example of a godly woman whose relationships were a loving conduit of grace and godly instruction. Like the Proverbs 31 woman, Naomi's influence was centered in her home, but Naomi's faith impacted women far beyond Israel's border. Her experiences show how God works through the close bonds of love—but Naomi's life adds the perspective that even godly relationships face roads of tragedy and sorrow.

NAOMI

Even in great hardship, Naomi nurtured her Moabite daughter-in-law, who became a believer—and an ancestor of Christ.

Before the time of King David, Bethlehem suffered a tremendous famine, and Naomi's family fled to the foreign land of Moab in search of food. While in Moab, Naomi's two sons married Moabite women, but within ten years, Naomi's husband and both of her sons had died. Now they were a family of three widows.

At just the right time, the famine ended and we see a fork in the road with the future of these women at stake. In that moment, we see the fruit and influence of Naomi's nurturing love. Tears flow, tender words are spoken, and the parting seems unbearable. One daughter-in-law returns to Moab, but the other, Ruth, makes a vow to follow Israel's God and stay with Naomi.

How important was it that Naomi shared her faith with Ruth? What was God's plan as He worked through Naomi's love? Ruth is in the family tree of Christ.

Neither Naomi nor Ruth could have imagined what God would do through their love and common faith. They simply walked together in faith, sharing sorrows, joys, and trust in their unfailing God. This same God also walks with you, working out His holy purposes in your life. He wants to love others through you.

4. Is there a place outside your comfort zone that God would like you to love others?

Mary, the mother of Jesus, had one of the most important relationships recorded in Scripture—she was the mother of the Savior.

MARY

"From now on all generations will call me blessed."

Mary was chosen by God in eternity to bear the promised Messiah. She carried the eternal God in her womb and raised Him as a child. Mary was blessed to be the mother of God's only Son.

Christ became true man, born of Mary. What an honor to serve the Lord in this role.

But the greatest relationship given to Mary was not between a son and his mother—it was Redeemer and redeemed.

With the Savior who would fulfill God's plan of salvation in her womb, Mary praised God for keeping His promises. Filled with the Spirit and the incarnate Christ, she burst into song, *"My soul magnifies the Lord and my spirit rejoices in God my Savior"* (Luke 1:46-47). Her thoughts are captured in Luke's Gospel, where we read that she *"treasured up all these things and pondered them in her heart"* (Luke 2:19). Mary loved and cared for Jesus throughout His earthly life because she knew He was the Savior. Her response to God's faithfulness was to love and serve Christ—and she had the privilege of starting in her own home.

So do you.

Mary did not do these things perfectly, nor can we. We need a Savior from sin because we fail at loving and serving others in our relationships. But with forgiveness and thanksgiving we can pattern our lives with this same attitude of trust, love, and service. It will look a lot like Mary and the Proverbs 31 woman.

But most of all, it will look like Jesus.

5. Compare the verses in this lesson to what you know about Mary's life and notice what similarities you find.

Living in Godly Wisdom — As I Influence Others in My Relationships

Scripture records the stories of many relationships. Some were blessed with joy and fulfillment—others were wrought with struggles and hardships. As you bear God's image in the world, your relationships will also bring both joy and sadness. But those relationships are an important opportunity for you to bear the image of God to others. They are relationships with a purpose.

Proverbs 31 refers to many relationships in the home and community, and the positive impact of those relationships is clear. This woman piques our curiosity because we want to build God-pleasing relationships. God's image is reflected in us as we mirror His love for people. It is a holy desire.

Our desire for relationships goes all the way back to God's design in the Garden. When the Lord announced, *"It is not good for the man to be alone"* (Genesis 2:18), He did not mean that everyone should be married. He *did* mean that men and women are designed differently—and we need each other. The family of God is filled with many relationships that nurture faith, speak truth, give help, and offer encouragement.

PAUL DAVID TRIPP

The biblical fact of the matter is that you were made for relationships.

Proverbs 31 shows us the blessing of relationships, but it never suggests we are insecure or incomplete without them. When we are content in God's perfect love, we are richly equipped to build relationships with others. Forgiveness, kindness, and love naturally deepen relationships. Helpful service builds trust and gratitude.

But God is also honored as we enjoy the simple blessing of companionship—because He created us to love others.

6. Think of someone who has influenced you, describe their impact, and determine how you can follow their example.

7. How can you model the relationships of the Proverbs 31 woman in your community (outside your home and church)?

Living in Godly Wisdom — As the Church Builds Relationships

The church encourages and strengthens believers. This is the primary relationship it nurtures—between a holy God and His redeemed children.

But God's chosen children are also placed into His family and united in faith with holiness and love. As Christians come together in worship, fellowship, and ministry, they build one another up and enjoy godly relationships. God allows us to learn more about those relationships in Proverbs 31.

The first glimpse we see is a personal and trusting relationship that brings great enrichment. Although the direct application is a marriage relationship, you can also see this as a relationship between a pastor and a church member, a Christian principal and a student, or a youth group leader and a struggling teen. You can see committed, self-sacrificing love that serves others with spiritual leadership—it is personal, trusting, and nurturing. It shares the truth and hope of the Word.

God intends these relationships to express His love and bring His help. We are His hands—His ambassadors to share and show grace.

Proverbs 31 sets these relationships in the context of a home, and we can easily see the parallel to the church. The commitment, self-sacrifice, and respect shown here give us a striking picture of how God's family can love each other. Scripture tells us to make *"every effort to keep the unity of the Spirit through the bond of peace"* (Ephesians 4:3). God's command is crystal clear. He wants His children to be a family and live together in love.

We will fail at these relationships because of sin, but the grace that unites us also washes us clean and compels us to try again. The Word of God equips and strengthens us to live in relationships that will draw others to see His goodness. This ripple of loving relationships extends far beyond the walls of the church into homes and communities throughout the world. The truth proclaimed in God's house equips and motivates us to nurture relationships everywhere.

That's the plan.

Share God's love and His completed plan of salvation with others.

Delight in Her Love – Her Relationships

Heavenly Father,

How deeply I rest in the arms of your love. The certainty of your faithful mercy fills my soul and comforts my heart. No other love can bring such joy and fullness. Let the promise of your everlasting love keep my heart content—and let your unfailing companionship move me to love others. Compelled by your love, guide me in relationships that will help others know the fullness of your grace. Give me your eyes to see others as you see them—and to love them with your love. Urge me to make every effort to build others up even when it's hard—even when it's painful. Teach me to be humble—and empty me of the pride that undermines and destroys relationships. May I do this for your glory as I serve you in everlasting righteousness, innocence, and blessedness. **Amen.**

Things to Remember and Pray About:

Proverbs 31

LIVING IN GODLY WISDOM: LESSON FOUR

Watch Her Serve   **Her Tasks**

Here comes the bewildering part: this woman works hard—and she works a lot.

But don't miss the wisdom here because you already work hard. Don't sigh when you see her long days and rolled up sleeves. Delight in her eager hands and willing heart as she demonstrates Solomon's wisdom, *"Whatever [you] do, do it with all your strength"* (Ecclesiastes 9:10, EHV). Rejoice in her skill and excitement as a woman of God who is *"eager to do what is good"* (Titus 2:14). Smile at her energy as it keeps pace with Paul's command to *"keep your spiritual fervor, serving the Lord"* (Romans 12:11). Then pause and beg for a balance of wisdom because we can't do it all—and God isn't saying we should. God isn't drawing attention to her active *hands*—He is highlighting her active *faith*.

Remember, this is her scrapbook, not her day planner.

The wisdom of Proverbs 31 refines our priorities and builds our trust in the Creator who uniquely designed us for His holy purposes. What abilities have you been given? What people need your kindness or help? In what moment can you share God's grace? Can you develop your God-given skills? What new things would you like to try? God gives us holy desires and leads us to people and places where we can be His hands and voice. When our skills and service are needed, we think about God's image in us and His eager desire to help others through us. We remember how God wants to extend His love through us.

The imagery of a scrapbook helps us see that our answer might be, "Now isn't the best time." It frees us from guilt and points us to God's wisdom as we make decisions—we are guarded against thinking, "I must." The various glimpses of this woman's life remind us how God works through all our service—but it also shows us God pleasing priorities. It helps us choose wisely on every page of life.

Watch Her Serve – Her Tasks

These verses deepen our wisdom as we see a living example of an entire life that is filled with eager hard work, personal skills, and compassionate service. Listen to God as He points to each page and reminisces . . .

Proverbs 31:13

- *She selects wool and flax and works with eager hands. (NIV)*
- *She looks for wool and flax and works with her hands in delight. (NASB)*
- *She looks for wool and flax and likes to work with her hands. (NCV)*
- *She seeks out wool and flax; she works joyfully with her hands. (CEB)*

Proverbs 31:15

- *She gets up while it is still night; she provides food for her family and portions for her female servants. (NIV)*
- *She's up before dawn, preparing breakfast for her family and organizing her day. (MSG)*

Proverbs 31:17

- *She sets about her work vigorously; her arms are strong for her tasks. (NIV)*
- *She works energetically; her arms are powerful. (CEB)*
- *First thing in the morning, she dresses for work, rolls up her sleeves, eager to get started. (MSG)*

Proverbs 31:19

- *In her hand she holds the distaff and grasps the spindle with her fingers. (NIV)*
- *She spins her own thread and weaves her own cloth. (GNT)*

Proverbs 31:20

- *She opens her arms to the poor and extends her hands to the needy. (NIV)*
- *She reaches out to the needy; she stretches out her hands to the poor. (CEB)*

Proverbs 31:22

- *She makes coverings for her bed; she is clothed in fine linen and purple. (NIV)*
- *She makes coverings for herself; her clothes are made of linen and other expensive material. (NCV)*
- *She makes quilts for herself. Her clothes are made of linen and purple cloth. (GW)*

Text Notes:

Verse 13 points to this woman's eagerness and willingness to work. It emphasizes the idea that she serves joyfully and loves what she is doing.

She gets up early and starts her day mindful of what others need. She is willing to give of herself or make sacrifices to help others succeed.

Don't miss the verbs in verse 20. She extends, reaches, and stretches—this isn't a casual effort. This woman goes out of her way to help people in need.

Many of these tasks are mundane and necessary, but she embraces them with joy because they express her love and faith. She spins the thread, weaves the cloth, and (in verse 24) makes the garments. Beginning to end, she does it all.

Her purple linen clothing is a mark of dignity but isn't an excessive luxury. She is adorned with inner beauty and God's Spirit, but she also wears clothes that are lovely, respectable, and modest.

This description brings to mind an amazing woman who lived 2,500 years later—Katie Luther. While Martin Luther was translating the Bible and reforming the Christian church, his wife Katie provided meals and hospitality to countless guests and students. Her strong arms and ability to work the land or care for the animals made her a tremendous blessing to Luther. Her companionship and help were life-changing gifts to him.

1. Discuss the abilities and interests God has given you. Where have you had the opportunity to use or develop your natural gifts and skills?

2. What wisdom can you glean from Jesus' words, *"Whatever you did for one of the least of these brothers and sisters of mine, you did for me"* (Matthew 25:40)?

3. When God sees all your work and the attitude in your heart, does it make you feel guilty or delighted?

Watch Her Serve – Her Tasks

Scripture Snapshots — Ruth and Dorcas

If there is one woman in Scripture who exemplifies hard work, strong arms, and willing service, it would be Ruth.

You may remember Ruth as the woman who became a widow in the land of Moab. She left her homeland and followed her mother-in-law Naomi to Bethlehem. Ruth wanted to remain in God's family and be a part of His holy nation, Israel. She could not have imagined what an important part of God's family she would be—she became an ancestor of Christ.

RUTH

Boaz and the townspeople marveled at Ruth's sacrifice, commitment, and hard work to support Naomi.

But you may not remember the time Ruth spent in the fields of Bethlehem, gathering grain through the barley and wheat seasons. She picked up grain left behind by the harvesters to provide for herself and Naomi. Her physical labor was demanding, but she was blessed as she worked in the fields of a distant relative.

Scripture etches Ruth's labors with high praise, and those who lived in Bethlehem took note of her sacrifices and commitment to Naomi. Her hard work didn't go unnoticed—especially by the owner of the fields, Boaz, who eventually took Ruth as his wife.

The grace and blessings given to Ruth were not a reward—she didn't work her way into God's favor or the heart of Boaz. Her life points to God's mercy. Her journey shows us that God works through our lives for His purposes and glory—even in times of trials or hardships.

4. What attitudes do you struggle with when you face hard work—and does the expectation of a reward or success ever creep into your thinking?

The New Testament also records the deeds of a godly woman who was praised and beloved by those around her. Her name was Dorcas. She was *"always doing good and helping the poor"* (Acts 9:36).

Acts 9:39 records how Peter was called to the town of Lydda after Dorcas had died. *"All the widows stood around him, crying and showing him the robes and other clothing that Dorcas had made while she was still with them."* Peter raised Dorcas from the dead and then *"called for the believers, especially the widows, and presented her to them alive"* (Acts 9:41).

> **DORCAS**
>
> *Moved by compassion, it was the men of the church who sent for Peter, urging him to come after Dorcas died.*

The witness Dorcas leaves is remarkable.

Her gifted service to Christ was radiant as she sewed clothes to help other women. Imagine what that looked like in the first century church when there were no department or fabric stores. Her garments were treasured—you can see it in this account from the book of Acts!

Do you envision her as a quiet, gentle woman who simply brought garments to church and dropped them off for women in need? Maybe. She may also have been a dynamic, outgoing woman bubbling with joy. Scripture points to the acts of faith, not the prominence or personality of the believer. He uses us all.

The key takeaway here is that Dorcas's service was an act of faith. Whether through quiet, behind-the-scenes work or a dynamic influence, love for God and others is active. Amy Carmichael said, "You can give without loving, but you can't love without giving." Each of us has opportunities to serve.

5. Think of the women in your church who serve others. How can you affirm their service and acts of faith?

Living in Godly Wisdom — As I Serve Others

The stories of these women are written so *"we might have hope"* (Romans 15:4).

Yes, we fail and hear the reminder that we need a Savior. That is good. But the tasks listed here are also a refreshing reminder that all our service honors God. Whatever we do, we can *"do it all in the name of the Lord Jesus, giving thanks to God the Father through him"* (Colossians 3:17). Every act of faith is beautiful. Every gift is needed. The body of Christ is filled as every part does its work.

God has a deliberate plan—and has distributed specific gifts to each believer accordingly. *"Now to each one the manifestation of the Spirit is given for the common good. . . . [11] All these are the work of one and the same Spirit, and he distributes them to each one, just as he determines"* (1 Co. 12:7, 11).

Don't undervalue your service. Don't live in continual guilt under the law. Study Scripture to learn more about God's gifts and plans for His people. Pay attention to where He has placed you and look for the opportunities He puts in your path for relationships and service.

GENE VEITH, JR.

The priesthood of all believers did not make everyone into church workers; rather, it turned every kind of work into a sacred calling.

What does that look like today?

It looks like Christian foster parents, classroom aides, EMT volunteers, and counselors. It looks like people who work with disadvantaged, elderly, or homeless people. It looks like honest employees and hard workers. It looks like people who love others and expect nothing in return—serving their families, employers, and communities for God's glory. It looks like a body of believers eagerly searching for places to use their gifts in a way that shows love and points others to Christ.

6. How does this lesson equip you for times when you can't see the impact of your service?

7. How can you help those around you see the godly purpose and value of their service or work?

Living in Godly Wisdom — As the Church Serves in Ministry

We've learned about the image of Christ in the church and the loving relationships that flow from our reconciliation with God. Now we see acts of service that begin at home and flourish in the church and community. This is the Bride of Christ—a holy family that loves others and serves for the glory of God and the growth of His Kingdom.

We call the work of the church "ministry," which simply means "service." The value of the Proverbs 31 woman doesn't come from her service, nor is the Bride of Christ valuable because of ministry work. Instead, we see how ministry and service extend the help and love of God to others. The church knows that the greatest, most loving "help" God offers is the forgiveness of sins—she never loses sight of that gift.

Strengthened in worship, believers are equipped and moved to action with grace, love, and a passion for souls. Outreach efforts and evangelism work become a priority as the Spirit urges believers with a holy desire to share His grace. The church unites to support mission work, ministry projects, and Christian education.

Christ continues to work through His children in daily living. He makes every task and act of service a work of faith. There is no distinction between church work and secular service because Christ purchased every believer with His blood. Every good thing they do glorifies God because they belong to Him. They bear His name and holy image in the world. This same Christian living is evident in Proverbs 31. This woman is eager and willing to serve in every area of life. She makes selfless sacrifices for others, mindful of those around her who need God's grace. And this is also a picture of the church.

But the willing attitude of the church and the Proverbs 31 woman is only a dim reflection of our Savior's perfect willingness as Jesus *"made himself nothing by taking the very nature of a servant"* (Philippians 2:7). Believers compelled to make sacrifices for others only give us a tiny glimpse of our Savior who *"humbled himself by becoming obedient to death—even death on a cross"* (Philippians 2:8).

Because of Christ's perfect, completed work of salvation, God does not demand any works or acts of service from His children.

With Christ's perfect work of salvation, the church is able to fill the world with truth, love, and endless acts of service that extend God's grace.

My Dear Servant-Savior,

Put before my eyes your perfect obedience that has completed all works of righteousness needed for my salvation. Set my confidence on the holy life you lived for me. Point me to your glorious resurrection that confirmed God's finished work of salvation. Then, in joy, let me serve you with every moment of my life and every ounce of my energy. Let this be the continual desire of my heart. Oh Lord, I confess that I fall short. I know that I lack energy, desire, and commitment—the verses of this chapter bring me more condemnation than comfort! But I know you paid for my sins and the Gospel has set me free! Now I can live for you and know that all my works are made holy because of you! Let your love always motivate me to serve you by serving others for your glory. **Amen.**

Things to Remember and Pray About:

Proverbs 31

LIVING IN GODLY WISDOM: LESSON FIVE

Follow Her Lead — Her Opportunities

With His inspired Word, God shows us the many ways He works in and through the lives of women. In Proverbs 31 God reveals a remarkable and beautiful Christian woman with a gift of leadership.

The incredible amount and diversity of work listed here confirms these are seasons of her life, not her daily tasks. But without doubt she uses her skills, intellect, and opportunities to be successful. In her home, real estate developments, and the marketplace, she does exceptional work. She researches an investment, plans profit margins, and manages finances for the glory of God. Her skills, abilities, and gifts of leadership are knit together by God with plans of a hope-filled future and a Christ-centered purpose.

But society pays no regard to the Savior who compels the Proverbs 31 woman to serve well. Even as she seeks to use her God-given gifts, the workplace can be brutal. Our disfigured world chafes against every glimpse of God's image. Places of influence are marred by mistrust, jealousy, and ingratitude. Selfish leaders and the demands of work can create an unbearable strain in family relationships. But God shows us this woman working to use her gifts, serve her family, and honor God. Why? Not to prove that she can do it or to set an expectation, but to give us visible hope and a compelling reminder of how God works through us to extend His love in the world.

Many Christian women will relate to these verses about the Proverbs 31 woman, especially as we consider the work she does outside her home. Women use their skills in courtrooms, classrooms, hospitals, and administrative offices—with weighty responsibilities that are managed for the glory of God. They work hard at their jobs because they are serving *"in the name of the Lord Jesus"* (Colossians 3:17). Rejoice at the many ways that women live for God's glory.

Follow Her Lead – Her Opportunities

These verses cover a lifetime of work done for the glory of God. Imagine the joy in her heart as she thanks God for these opportunities.

Proverbs 31:14

- *She is like the ships of the merchant; she brings her food from afar. (ESV)*
- *She's like a trading ship that sails to faraway places and brings back exotic surprises. (MSG)*

Proverbs 31:16

- *She considers a field and buys it; out of her earnings she plants a vineyard. (NIV)*
- *She evaluates a field and buys it; she plants a vineyard with her earnings. (HCSB)*
- *She surveys a field and acquires it; from her own resources, she plants a vineyard. (CEB)*

Proverbs 31:18

- *She sees that her trading is profitable, and her lamp does not go out at night. (NIV)*
- *She makes sure her dealings are profitable; her lamp burns late into the night. (NLT)*

Proverbs 31:21

- *When it snows, she has no fear for her household; for all of them are clothed in scarlet. (NIV)*
- *She doesn't fear for her household when it snows, because they are all dressed in warm clothes. (CEB)*
- *She does not fear for her family when it snows because her whole family has a double layer of clothing. (GW)*

Proverbs 31:24

- *She makes linen garments and sells them, and supplies the merchants with sashes. (NIV)*
- *She makes clothes to sell to the shop owners. (CEV)*

Proverbs 31:27

- *She watches over the activities of her household and is never idle. (HCSB)*
- *She watches over her family and never wastes her time. (NCV)*

Text Notes:

The idea of a *"merchant ship"* is easily lost in our world of modern shipping. *Rules of Civility* by Amor Towles captures the picture of verse 14 perfectly.

> In the center of the table was a bowl of fruits so well-to-do that half of them I'd never seen before. There was a small green furry sphere. A yellow succulent that looked like a miniature football. To get to Anne's table, they must have traveled farther than I had traveled in my entire life. (p. 255)

You might be surprised by the reference to snow in Proverbs 31, but don't imagine it like a Midwestern snowstorm. Instead, the point is that she doesn't live in fear when she sees the possibility of danger. Her children have what they need because God has used her to wisely clothe them. They are secure. Think of how this imagery parallels the robe of righteousness given in Baptism. Hear it echo the truth that God's Word strengthens and defends us against all danger! It isn't her work or her efforts that give her confidence but the certain assurance of God's faithfulness.

Her management skills are extraordinary. Whether she's balancing her checkbook, planning her harvest, or making sure the family chores are done, she is wise and insightful. God says this gifted businesswoman is *"noble"* (Proverbs 31:10). These are His words and His description.

1. This woman is affirmed by her husband in Proverbs 31:11, 23, 28. How do you think he supports his wife's leadership opportunities?

2. Based on what you've learned about this woman's character, what do you think her leadership would be like?

3. Discuss the frustrations you've experienced when your leadership doesn't seem successful.

Follow Her Lead – Her Opportunities

Scripture Snapshots — Deborah and Lydia

Long ago, before King David ruled Israel, God's people were led by judges. During this time, Israel consistently faltered and was unfaithful to the Lord. *"Everyone did as they saw fit"* (Judges 17:6). There is little in the book of Judges that would trigger admiration for God's people—but we see God's guidance, power, and faithfulness just the same. It was during this dismal time that Deborah was a judge and leader in Israel.

As a civil judge, Deborah settled disputes from her court in the hill country under a tree called *"The Palm of Deborah"* (Judges 4:5).

As a prophetess who spoke God's truth, she faithfully repeated the message God gave her for Israel's commander.

> **DEBORAH**
>
> *The Lord sent Deborah a message for Barak to gather Israel's men and fight against the powerful army of Canaan.*

Israel had been cruelly oppressed for twenty years by the wicked king of Canaan. His vicious commander, Sisera (**sis**-eh-ra) had nine hundred chariots fitted with iron. God's people had been stripped of their weapons, strength, and hope. But God heard their cry and was ready to respond.

God gave Deborah a message for Barak, the commander of Israel's army.

She called for Barak and delivered God's command. Though Barak needed Deborah's continual encouragement, he rallied 10,000 men on Mount Tabor to fight for Israel. They descended toward a seemingly hopeless battle, but the Lord sent rain, causing the Canaanite chariots to get stuck in the mud. Israel prevailed, and the victory song of Deborah and Barak is written in Judges chapter five.

Deborah's civil leadership, spiritual obedience, and encouragement to Barak is radiant with respect and dignity. Her story is important to women as they seek to honor God in secular service with Biblical wisdom and integrity. Her account isn't a trump card that proves a point—it refines our wisdom for relationships in a sinful world and builds trust as God powerfully intervenes for His people.

4. What important or unique actions did you note in Deborah's life?

Lydia was a businesswoman in ancient Philippi. Though she was a Gentile, she believed in the God of Israel and trusted His promises.

LYDIA

Lydia, a "seller of purple cloth," became a believer when Paul first arrived in Philippi. The church met in her home, and her hospitality was a refuge for Paul.

On the Sabbath, Lydia joined the Jewish women by the river in Philippi to worship. When Paul arrived to share the message of Christ, Lydia was one of the first people to hear the Gospel on the continent of Europe. Luke records the conversion and baptism of Lydia and her household.

Afterward, Luke continues, *"She begged us, saying, 'If you have judged me to be faithful to the Lord, come to my house and stay.' So she persuaded us"* (Acts 16:15).

Lydia reflects the beauty and strength of Christian leadership and service as she responds to the Gospel. She takes the initiative to invite Paul and his companions to her home, where she accommodates worship and ministry for the new church in Philippi. Her home also became a refuge for Paul and Silas when they were later released from prison (Acts 16:40).

Lydia's God-given gifts, skills, and resources as a businesswoman would have been a great blessing to this growing congregation. It is interesting to think of Lydia's hospitality and support for ministry when Paul writes about the generosity of the Philippian church, *"You sent me aid more than once when I was in need"* (Philippians 4:16).

Scripture paints Lydia in a beautiful light as a believer much like the woman in Proverbs 31. Lydia's strengths and generous hospitality, woven with her love for Christ, make her a wonderful example. She encourages us to remember that God helps each person balance the responsibilities of family, work, and service to others as they are guided by God's wisdom.

5. How do the similarities between Deborah, Lydia, and the Proverbs 31 woman give you encouragement?

Follow Her Lead – Her Opportunities

Living in Godly Wisdom — As I Accept Leadership

The truth of Scripture and godly examples of women in leadership give us hope and direction as we live for Christ in the secular world. People need to see the image of God in the workplace, they ache for the Lord's kindness in relationships, and they marvel at selfless service in leadership. These traits are desperately needed in a world that is dark and confused—and God gives believers many gifts and opportunities to advance the Gospel.

Women traverse a lot of thoughts, priorities, and emotions as they make choices about career opportunities and leadership. Where can I best bear God's image? How will this impact my relationships and family? Is this a good use of God's gifts and the best investment of my time? Scripture gives guidance, wisdom, and strength for godly decisions—but it doesn't give easy answers. God highlights His priorities, but believers prayerfully manage their gifts and circumstances. They study Scripture for insight and listen for the wisdom of fellow believers. Then they make the best decision they can and pray to be shining examples of God's image.

> **SHAUNA NIEQUIST**
>
> *The best thing I can offer to this world is not my force or energy, but a well-tended spirit, a wise and brave soul.*

Your job—every job—is an opportunity to demonstrate God's love and forgiveness. It isn't just leadership that honors God—we have clearly established that all service honors Him. But if you have been entrusted with a position of leadership, it will be a place to honor God with truth, godly priorities, and wisdom. Lead with confidence and humility that reflect Christ and bear His image. Let authority and orderliness bring God respect and glory. Don't fall into the temptation of pride or worldly gain but work to the best of your ability, knowing God will use your gifts according to His divine purposes. Trust Him to work in you and through you.

6. What key qualities are important in Christian leaders?

7. How do you stay focused on the highest calling—that of faith?

Living in Godly Wisdom — As the Church Offers Leadership

The church is a shining example of Christ's selfless leadership as it looks to the good of others in proclaiming the Gospel in the Word and sacraments.

Like the merchant ship that travels to bring good gifts, the church brings the Gospel to all nations. *"Variety"* and *"novelty"* are evident in the ways we communicate the Gospel. Every time we cross a cultural or generational border to share the message of Christ, we are a merchant ship bringing the hope of eternal life. The doors and opportunities for ministry in congregations are as varied as God's people.

Like the Proverbs 31 woman who considers a field and plants a vineyard, churches prayerfully consider ministry opportunities and look for places to spread the seeds of God's truth. Churches employ thoughtful strategy as they seek to use their gifts in the best possible way.

Like the examples we have studied, churches work in an orderly way that serves the greater good. Leaders in the church rely on Scripture and follow God's direction. God calls the brothers in the family to take responsibility for preaching the Word and providing spiritual oversight that will benefit others. He commands those men to reflect Christ's selfless love for the church, equip believers with the Word, and make sacrifices for the good of the church.

With godly partnerships that value every person and honor every gift, the church thrives like the woman in Proverbs 31. God's image, healthy relationships, selfless service, and Christ-like leadership will adorn the church with beauty and dignity. The power of Word and sacraments will motivate and guide men and women to work together in humility, love, and respect according to His design.

This is God's church—and she is radiant with His glory.

Follow Her Lead – Her Opportunities

Lord God,

You have planned and worked salvation for your people, and you continue to give us opportunities to live in faith for your good purposes. We tremble at the truth that you work in and through us—we are humbled and thankful for this holy privilege. Keep us mindful of that honor—and make us both willing and wise in our service. Guide us in our decision-making and bless the work of our hands. Make our leadership and example in the world a reflection of your image with relationships and service that will draw others to you. Thank you for pastors and leaders who faithfully proclaim your truth and give spiritual oversight that benefits and equips all people. We pray that you would use all our gifts and opportunities to share Christ with the world. Strengthen us all with a desire to seek your honor as we proclaim the truth of salvation in Christ. **Amen.**

Things to Remember and Pray About:

Final Thoughts — A Summary

In the past, you may have seen the Proverbs 31 woman as an intimidating, overworked, and unrelatable person. When the guilt of the law guides your view of her, she *is* condemning and alienating. We may withdraw and close our hearts to the message of God because we see only our failures.

Praise God for the saving work of Christ and His forgiveness.

With eyes of faith, you can see the Proverbs 31 woman as a loving, encouraging sister who reflects God's image in her daily living. She serves with energy and integrity. You can praise God for her gifts and be thankful for all she does. You can visualize how we are called to serve and walk together in faith for God's glory. Her relationships are fertile ground for godly love and Christian witness.

Now that you see her with those eyes, God encourages you to look around and see your sisters in Christ the same way. Set aside the intimidations and irritations—put off the jealousy and envy that taint your view of others. Don't let your sinful flesh create separation and enmity where God wants love and harmony. Live at peace with your sisters in Christ.

See your brothers in Christ as family members who love and need you. Respect their spiritual leadership, unique qualities, and loving service as you work together for God's Kingdom. Live in partnerships that rejoice in our common callings as believers and uphold the unique callings God gives to men and women.

As believers are united in His Spirit and view one another with eyes of faith, the body of Christ will grow. The church of Christ will flourish. The world will see the image of God more clearly and be amazed at our loving, self-sacrificing relationships. Service will abound in humility. Leadership will always look to the good of others. Every part of the body of Christ will do its part according to its purpose.

This beautiful picture of a godly woman is clear and compelling. Shining in the pages of Scripture, God has given a remarkable guide for women as they live in response to the Gospel.

May God's Word strengthen you to live it well.

Proverbs 31:10-31 in a variety of translations

Proverbs 31

CEB - Common English Bible

The competent wife

¹⁰ A competent wife, how does one find her?
   Her value is far above pearls.
¹¹ Her husband entrusts his heart to her,
   and with her he will have all he needs.
¹² She brings him good and not trouble
   all the days of her life.
¹³ She seeks out wool and flax;
   she works joyfully with her hands.
¹⁴ She is like a fleet of merchant ships,
   bringing food from a distance.
¹⁵ She gets up while it is still night,
   providing food for her household,
   even some for her female servants.
¹⁶ She surveys a field and acquires it;
   from her own resources, she plants a vineyard.
¹⁷ She works energetically;
   her arms are powerful.
¹⁸ She realizes that her trading is successful;
   she doesn't put out her lamp at night.
¹⁹ She puts her hands to the spindle;
   her palms grasp the whorl.
²⁰ She reaches out to the needy;
   she stretches out her hands to the poor.
²¹ She doesn't fear for her household when it snows,
   because they are all dressed in warm clothes.
²² She makes bedspreads for herself;
   fine linen and purple are her clothing.

²³ Her husband is known in the city gates
   when he sits with the elders of the land.
²⁴ She makes garments and sells them;
   she supplies sashes to traders.
²⁵ Strength and honor are her clothing;
   she is confident about the future.
²⁶ Her mouth is full of wisdom;
   kindly teaching is on her tongue.
²⁷ She is vigilant over the activities of her household;
   she doesn't eat the food of laziness.
²⁸ Her children bless her;
   her husband praises her:
²⁹   "Many women act competently,
   but you surpass them all!"
³⁰ Charm is deceptive and beauty fleeting,
   but a woman who fears the LORD is to be praised.
³¹ Let her share in the results of her work;
   let her deeds praise her in the city gates.

Proverbs 31:10-31 in a variety of translations

Proverbs 31

CEV - Contemporary English Version

In Praise of a Good Wife
¹⁰ A truly good wife
is the most precious treasure a man can find!
¹¹ Her husband depends on her,
   and she never lets him down.
¹² She is good to him
   every day of her life,
¹³   and with her own hands she gladly makes clothes.
¹⁴ She is like a sailing ship
   that brings food from across the sea.
¹⁵ She gets up before daylight
to prepare food for her family
   and for her servants.
¹⁶ She knows how to buy land
and how to plant a vineyard,
¹⁷   and she always works hard.
¹⁸ She knows when to buy or sell,
   and she stays busy until late at night.
¹⁹ She spins her own cloth,
²⁰   and she helps the poor and the needy.
²¹ Her family has warm clothing,
   and so she doesn't worry when it snows.
²² She does her own sewing,
   and everything she wears is beautiful.
²³ Her husband is a well-known
and respected leader in the city.

⁲⁴ She makes clothes to sell
   to the shop owners.
²⁵ She is strong and graceful,
   as well as cheerful about the future.
²⁶ Her words are sensible,
   and her advice is thoughtful.
²⁷ She takes good care
of her family and is never lazy.
²⁸ Her children praise her,
   and with great pride her husband says,
²⁹ "There are many good women,
   but you are the best!"
³⁰ Charm can be deceiving,
   and beauty fades away,
but a woman who honors the LORD
   deserves to be praised.
³¹ Show her respect—
   praise her in public for what she has done.

Proverbs 31:10-31 in a variety of translations

Proverbs 31

EHV – Evangelical Heritage Version

The Strong Wife

¹⁰ Who can find a wife with strong character?
Her value is greater than that of gems.
¹¹ Her husband's heart trusts her,
and he never lacks wealth.
¹² She does good for him and not evil
　all the days of her life.
¹³ She obtains wool and flax.
She eagerly works it with her hands.
¹⁴ She is like merchant ships.
She brings her food from far away.
¹⁵ She rises while it is still night.
She gives food to her household.
She gives their share to her female servants.
¹⁶ She considers a field and acquires it.
From her own income, she plants a vineyard.
¹⁷ She wraps strength around her waist like a belt,
and she makes her arms strong.
¹⁸ She realizes that she makes a good profit.
Her lamp does not go out at night.
¹⁹ She stretches out her hands for the distaff,
and the palms of her hands grasp the spindle.
²⁰ She opens the palm of her hand to the oppressed,
and she stretches out her hands to the needy.
²¹ She does not fear for her household on account of snow,
because her entire household is clothed in scarlet clothing.
²² She makes bedspreads for herself.
Fine linen and purple cloth are her clothing.
²³ Her husband is known at the city gates,
where he sits with the elders of the land.

*²⁴ She makes linen garments and sells them,
and she delivers belts to the merchants.
²⁵ Strength and honor are her clothing,
and she laughs at the days to come.
²⁶ She opens her mouth with wisdom,
and kind instruction is on her tongue.
²⁷ She keeps a close eye on the conduct of her household,
and she does not eat bread that she did not work for.
²⁸ Her children rise up and bless her.
Her husband rises up and praises her:
²⁹ "Many daughters show strong character,
but you have surpassed all of them."
³⁰ Charm is deceptive, and beauty is vapor that vanishes,
but a woman who fears the Lord should be praised.
³¹ Give her credit for the fruit of her hands,
and let her accomplishments praise her in the city gates.*

Proverbs 31

ESV – English Standard Version

The Woman Who Fears the LORD

¹⁰ An excellent wife who can find?
   She is far more precious than jewels.
¹¹ The heart of her husband trusts in her,
   and he will have no lack of gain.
¹² She does him good, and not harm,
   all the days of her life.
¹³ She seeks wool and flax,
   and works with willing hands.
¹⁴ She is like the ships of the merchant;
   she brings her food from afar.
¹⁵ She rises while it is yet night
   and provides food for her household
   and portions for her maidens.
¹⁶ She considers a field and buys it;
   with the fruit of her hands she plants a vineyard.
¹⁷ She dresses herself with strength
   and makes her arms strong.
¹⁸ She perceives that her merchandise is profitable.
   Her lamp does not go out at night.
¹⁹ She puts her hands to the distaff,
   and her hands hold the spindle.
²⁰ She opens her hand to the poor
   and reaches out her hands to the needy.
²¹ She is not afraid of snow for her household,
   for all her household are clothed in scarlet.

²² She makes bed coverings for herself;
    her clothing is fine linen and purple.
²³ Her husband is known in the gates
    when he sits among the elders of the land.
²⁴ She makes linen garments and sells them;
    she delivers sashes to the merchant.
²⁵ Strength and dignity are her clothing,
    and she laughs at the time to come.
²⁶ She opens her mouth with wisdom,
    and the teaching of kindness is on her tongue.
²⁷ She looks well to the ways of her household
    and does not eat the bread of idleness.
²⁸ Her children rise up and call her blessed;
    her husband also, and he praises her:
²⁹ "Many women have done excellently,
    but you surpass them all."
³⁰ Charm is deceitful, and beauty is vain,
    but a woman who fears the LORD is to be praised.
³¹ Give her of the fruit of her hands,
    and let her works praise her in the gates.

Proverbs 31:10-31 in a variety of translations

Proverbs 31

GNT – Good News Translation

The Capable Wife

¹⁰ How hard it is to find a capable wife! She is worth far more than jewels!
¹¹ Her husband puts his confidence in her, and he will never be poor.
¹² As long as she lives, she does him good and never harm.
¹³ She keeps herself busy making wool and linen cloth.
¹⁴ She brings home food from out-of-the-way places, as merchant ships do.
¹⁵ She gets up before daylight to prepare food for her family and to tell her servant women what to do.
¹⁶ She looks at land and buys it, and with money she has earned she plants a vineyard.
¹⁷ She is a hard worker, strong and industrious.
¹⁸ She knows the value of everything she makes, and works late into the night.
¹⁹ She spins her own thread and weaves her own cloth.
²⁰ She is generous to the poor and needy.
²¹ She doesn't worry when it snows, because her family has warm clothing.
²² She makes bedspreads and wears clothes of fine purple linen.
²³ Her husband is well known, one of the leading citizens.
²⁴ She makes clothes and belts, and sells them to merchants.
²⁵ She is strong and respected and not afraid of the future.
²⁶ She speaks with a gentle wisdom.
²⁷ She is always busy and looks after her family's needs.
²⁸ Her children show their appreciation, and her husband praises her.
²⁹ He says, "Many women are good wives, but you are the best of them all."
³⁰ Charm is deceptive and beauty disappears, but a woman who honors the LORD should be praised.
³¹ Give her credit for all she does. She deserves the respect of everyone.

Proverbs 31

GW – God's Word Translation

A Poem in Hebrew Alphabetical Order

¹⁰ "Who can find a wife with a strong character?
    She is worth far more than jewels.
¹¹ Her husband trusts her with all his heart,
    and he does not lack anything good.
¹² She helps him and never harms him all the days of her life.
¹³ "She seeks out wool and linen with care
    and works with willing hands.
¹⁴ She is like merchant ships.
    She brings her food from far away.
¹⁵ She wakes up while it is still dark
    and gives food to her family
        and portions of food to her female slaves.
¹⁶ "She picks out a field and buys it.
    She plants a vineyard from the profits she has earned.
¹⁷ She puts on strength like a belt
    and goes to work with energy.
¹⁸ She sees that she is making a good profit.
    Her lamp burns late at night.
¹⁹ "She puts her hands on the distaff,
    and her fingers hold a spindle.
²⁰ She opens her hands to oppressed people
    and stretches them out to needy people.
²¹ She does not fear for her family when it snows
    because her whole family
        has a double layer of clothing.
²² She makes quilts for herself.
    Her clothes are made of linen and purple cloth.

Proverbs 31:10-31 in a variety of translations

²³ "Her husband is known at the city gates
   when he sits with the leaders of the land.
²⁴ "She makes linen garments and sells them
   and delivers belts to the merchants.
²⁵ She dresses with strength and nobility,
   and she smiles at the future.
²⁶ "She speaks with wisdom,
   and on her tongue there is tender instruction.
²⁷ She keeps a close eye on the conduct of her family,
   and she does not eat the bread of idleness.
²⁸ Her children and her husband
   stand up and bless her.
   In addition, he sings her praises, by saying,
²⁹ 'Many women have done noble work,
   but you have surpassed them all!'
³⁰ "Charm is deceptive, and beauty evaporates,
   but a woman who has the fear of the Lord should be praised.
³¹ Reward her for what she has done,
   and let her achievements praise her at the city gates."

Proverbs 31

HCSB – Holman Christian Standard Bible

In Praise of a Capable Wife
¹⁰ Who can find a capable wife?
She is far more precious than jewels.
¹¹ The heart of her husband trusts in her,
and he will not lack anything good.
¹² She rewards him with good, not evil,
all the days of her life.
¹³ She selects wool and flax
and works with willing hands.
¹⁴ She is like the merchant ships,
bringing her food from far away.
¹⁵ She rises while it is still night
and provides food for her household
and portions for her female servants.
¹⁶ She evaluates a field and buys it;
she plants a vineyard with her earnings.
¹⁷ She draws on her strength
and reveals that her arms are strong.
¹⁸ She sees that her profits are good,
and her lamp never goes out at night.
¹⁹ She extends her hands to the spinning staff,
and her hands hold the spindle.
²⁰ Her hands reach out to the poor,
and she extends her hands to the needy.
²¹ She is not afraid for her household when it snows,
for all in her household are doubly clothed.
²² She makes her own bed coverings;
her clothing is fine linen and purple.
²³ Her husband is known at the city gates,

Proverbs 31:10-31 in a variety of translations

where he sits among the elders of the land.
²⁴ She makes and sells linen garments;
she delivers belts to the merchants.
²⁵ Strength and honor are her clothing,
and she can laugh at the time to come.
²⁶ She opens her mouth with wisdom
and loving instruction is on her tongue.
²⁷ She watches over the activities of her household
and is never idle.
²⁸ Her sons rise up and call her blessed.
Her husband also praises her:
²⁹ "Many women are capable,
but you surpass them all!"
³⁰ Charm is deceptive and beauty is fleeting,
but a woman who fears the LORD will be praised.
³¹ Give her the reward of her labor,
and let her works praise her at the city gates.

Proverbs 31

MSG – The Message

Hymn to a Good Wife

¹⁰⁻³¹ A good woman is hard to find,
  and worth far more than diamonds.
Her husband trusts her without reserve,
  and never has reason to regret it.
Never spiteful, she treats him generously
  all her life long.
She shops around for the best yarns and cottons,
  and enjoys knitting and sewing.
She's like a trading ship that sails to faraway places
  and brings back exotic surprises.
She's up before dawn, preparing breakfast
  for her family and organizing her day.
She looks over a field and buys it,
  then, with money she's put aside, plants a garden.
First thing in the morning, she dresses for work,
  rolls up her sleeves, eager to get started.
She senses the worth of her work,
  is in no hurry to call it quits for the day.
She's skilled in the crafts of home and hearth,
  diligent in homemaking.
She's quick to assist anyone in need,
  reaches out to help the poor.
She doesn't worry about her family when it snows;
  their winter clothes are all mended and ready to wear.
She makes her own clothing,
  and dresses in colorful linens and silks.
Her husband is greatly respected
  when he deliberates with the city fathers.
She designs gowns and sells them,
  brings the sweaters she knits to the dress shops.
Her clothes are well-made and elegant,

Proverbs 31:10-31 in a variety of translations

  and she always faces tomorrow with a smile.
When she speaks she has something worthwhile to say,
  and she always says it kindly.
She keeps an eye on everyone in her household,
  and keeps them all busy and productive.
Her children respect and bless her;
  her husband joins in with words of praise:
"Many women have done wonderful things,
  but you've outclassed them all!"
Charm can mislead and beauty soon fades.
  The woman to be admired and praised
  is the woman who lives in the Fear-of-GOD.
Give her everything she deserves!
  Adorn her life with praises!

Proverbs 31:10-31 in a variety of translations

Proverbs 31

NASB – New American Standard Bible

Description of a Worthy Woman

¹⁰ An excellent wife, who can find her?
For her worth is far above jewels.
¹¹ The heart of her husband trusts in her,
And he will have no lack of gain.
¹² She does him good and not evil
All the days of her life.
¹³ She looks for wool and linen,
And works with her hands in delight.
¹⁴ She is like merchant ships;
She brings her food from afar.
¹⁵ And she rises while it is still night
And gives food to her household,
And portions to her attendants.
¹⁶ She considers a field and buys it;
From her earnings she plants a vineyard.
¹⁷ She surrounds her waist with strength
And makes her arms strong.
¹⁸ She senses that her profit is good;
Her lamp does not go out at night.
¹⁹ She stretches out her hands to the distaff,
And her hands grasp the spindle.
²⁰ She extends her hand to the poor,
And she stretches out her hands to the needy.
²¹ She is not afraid of the snow for her household,
For all her household are clothed with scarlet.
²² She makes coverings for herself;
Her clothing is fine linen and purple.
²³ Her husband is known in the gates,
When he sits among the elders of the land.
²⁴ She makes linen garments and sells them,
And supplies belts to the tradesmen.

Proverbs 31:10-31 in a variety of translations

²⁵ Strength and dignity are her clothing,
And she smiles at the future.
²⁶ She opens her mouth in wisdom,
And the teaching of kindness is on her tongue.
²⁷ She watches over the activities of her household,
And does not eat the bread of idleness.
²⁸ Her children rise up and bless her;
Her husband also, and he praises her, saying:
²⁹ "Many daughters have done nobly,
But you excel them all."
³⁰ Charm is deceitful and beauty is vain,
But a woman who fears the LORD, she shall be praised.
³¹ Give her the product of her hands,
And let her works praise her in the gates.

Proverbs 31

NCV – New Century Version

The Good Wife

¹⁰ It is hard to find a good wife,
   because she is worth more than rubies.
¹¹ Her husband trusts her completely.
   With her, he has everything he needs.
¹² She does him good and not harm
   for as long as she lives.
¹³ She looks for wool and flax
   and likes to work with her hands.
¹⁴ She is like a trader's ship,
   bringing food from far away.
¹⁵ She gets up while it is still dark
   and prepares food for her family
   and feeds her servant girls.
¹⁶ She inspects a field and buys it.
   With money she earned, she plants a vineyard.
¹⁷ She does her work with energy,
   and her arms are strong.
¹⁸ She knows that what she makes is good.
   Her lamp burns late into the night.
¹⁹ She makes thread with her hands
   and weaves her own cloth.
²⁰ She welcomes the poor
   and helps the needy.
²¹ She does not worry about her family when it snows,
   because they all have fine clothes to keep them warm.
²² She makes coverings for herself;
   her clothes are made of linen and other expensive material.
²³ Her husband is known at the city meetings,
   where he makes decisions as one of the leaders of the land.

Proverbs 31:10-31 in a variety of translations

²⁴ *She makes linen clothes and sells them*
   and provides belts to the merchants.
²⁵ *She is strong and is respected by the people.*
   She looks forward to the future with joy.
²⁶ *She speaks wise words*
   and teaches others to be kind.
²⁷ *She watches over her family*
   and never wastes her time.
²⁸ *Her children speak well of her.*
   Her husband also praises her,
²⁹ *saying, "There are many fine women,*
   but you are better than all of them."
³⁰ *Charm can fool you, and beauty can trick you,*
   but a woman who respects the LORD should be praised.
³¹ *Give her the reward she has earned;*
   she should be praised in public for what she has done.

Proverbs 31

NIV – New International Version

Epilogue: The Wife of Noble Character

¹⁰ A wife of noble character who can find?
   She is worth far more than rubies.
¹¹ Her husband has full confidence in her
   and lacks nothing of value.
¹² She brings him good, not harm,
   all the days of her life.
¹³ She selects wool and flax
   and works with eager hands.
¹⁴ She is like the merchant ships,
   bringing her food from afar.
¹⁵ She gets up while it is still night;
   she provides food for her family
   and portions for her female servants.
¹⁶ She considers a field and buys it;
   out of her earnings she plants a vineyard.
¹⁷ She sets about her work vigorously;
   her arms are strong for her tasks.
¹⁸ She sees that her trading is profitable,
   and her lamp does not go out at night.
¹⁹ In her hand she holds the distaff
   and grasps the spindle with her fingers.
²⁰ She opens her arms to the poor
   and extends her hands to the needy.
²¹ When it snows, she has no fear for her household;
   for all of them are clothed in scarlet.
²² She makes coverings for her bed;
   she is clothed in fine linen and purple.
²³ Her husband is respected at the city gate,
   where he takes his seat among the elders of the land.

Proverbs 31:10-31 in a variety of translations

²⁴ She makes linen garments and sells them,
   and supplies the merchants with sashes.
²⁵ She is clothed with strength and dignity;
   she can laugh at the days to come.
²⁶ She speaks with wisdom,
   and faithful instruction is on her tongue.
²⁷ She watches over the affairs of her household
   and does not eat the bread of idleness.
²⁸ Her children arise and call her blessed;
   her husband also, and he praises her:
²⁹ "Many women do noble things,
   but you surpass them all."
³⁰ Charm is deceptive, and beauty is fleeting;
   but a woman who fears the LORD is to be praised.
³¹ Honor her for all that her hands have done,
   and let her works bring her praise at the city gate.

Proverbs 31

NKJV – New King James Version

The Virtuous Wife

^{10} Who can find a virtuous wife?
For her worth is far above rubies.
^{11} The heart of her husband safely trusts her;
So he will have no lack of gain.
^{12} She does him good and not evil
All the days of her life.
^{13} She seeks wool and flax,
And willingly works with her hands.
^{14} She is like the merchant ships,
She brings her food from afar.
^{15} She also rises while it is yet night,
And provides food for her household,
And a portion for her maidservants.
^{16} She considers a field and buys it;
From her profits she plants a vineyard.
^{17} She girds herself with strength,
And strengthens her arms.
^{18} She perceives that her merchandise is good,
And her lamp does not go out by night.
^{19} She stretches out her hands to the distaff,
And her hand holds the spindle.
^{20} She extends her hand to the poor,
Yes, she reaches out her hands to the needy.
^{21} She is not afraid of snow for her household,
For all her household is clothed with scarlet.
^{22} She makes tapestry for herself;
Her clothing is fine linen and purple.
^{23} Her husband is known in the gates,
When he sits among the elders of the land.
^{24} She makes linen garments and sells them,

Proverbs 31:10-31 in a variety of translations

And supplies sashes for the merchants.
^{25} Strength and honor are her clothing;
She shall rejoice in time to come.
^{26} She opens her mouth with wisdom,
And on her tongue is the law of kindness.
^{27} She watches over the ways of her household,
And does not eat the bread of idleness.
^{28} Her children rise up and call her blessed;
Her husband also, and he praises her:
^{29} "Many daughters have done well,
But you excel them all."
^{30} Charm is deceitful and beauty is passing,
But a woman who fears the LORD, she shall be praised.
^{31} Give her of the fruit of her hands,
And let her own works praise her in the gates.

Proverbs 31:10-31 in a variety of translations

Proverbs 31

NLT – New Living Translation

A Wife of Noble Character

¹⁰ Who can find a virtuous and capable wife?
    She is more precious than rubies.
¹¹ Her husband can trust her,
    and she will greatly enrich his life.
¹² She brings him good, not harm,
    all the days of her life.
¹³ She finds wool and flax
    and busily spins it.
¹⁴ She is like a merchant's ship,
    bringing her food from afar.
¹⁵ She gets up before dawn to prepare breakfast for her household
    and plan the day's work for her servant girls.
¹⁶ She goes to inspect a field and buys it;
    with her earnings she plants a vineyard.
¹⁷ She is energetic and strong,
    a hard worker.
¹⁸ She makes sure her dealings are profitable;
    her lamp burns late into the night.
¹⁹ Her hands are busy spinning thread,
    her fingers twisting fiber.
²⁰ She extends a helping hand to the poor
    and opens her arms to the needy.
²¹ She has no fear of winter for her household,
    for everyone has warm clothes.
²² She makes her own bedspreads.
    She dresses in fine linen and purple gowns.
²³ Her husband is well known at the city gates,
    where he sits with the other civic leaders.
²⁴ She makes belted linen garments
    and sashes to sell to the merchants.

Proverbs 31:10-31 in a variety of translations

²⁵ She is clothed with strength and dignity,
    and she laughs without fear of the future.
²⁶ When she speaks, her words are wise,
    and she gives instructions with kindness.
²⁷ She carefully watches everything in her household
    and suffers nothing from laziness.
²⁸ Her children stand and bless her.
    Her husband praises her:
²⁹ "There are many virtuous and capable women in the world,
    but you surpass them all!"
³⁰ Charm is deceptive, and beauty does not last;
    but a woman who fears the LORD will be greatly praised.
³¹ Reward her for all she has done.
    Let her deeds publicly declare her praise.

Proverbs 31:10-31 in a variety of translations

Proverbs 31

NLV – New Life Version

The Wisdom of King Lemuel's Mother

¹⁰ Who can find a good wife? For she is worth far more than rubies that make one rich. ¹¹ The heart of her husband trusts in her, and he will never stop getting good things. ¹² She does him good and not bad all the days of her life. ¹³ She looks for wool and flax, and works with willing hands. ¹⁴ She is like ships that trade. She brings her food from far away. ¹⁵ She rises while it is still night and makes food for all those in her house. She gives work for the young women to do. ¹⁶ She gives careful thought to a field and buys it. She plants grape-vines from what she has earned. ¹⁷ She makes herself ready with strength, and makes her arms strong. ¹⁸ She sees that what she has earned is good. Her lamp does not go out at night. ¹⁹ She puts her hands to the wheel to make cloth. ²⁰ She opens her hand to the poor, and holds out her hands to those in need. ²¹ She is not afraid of the snow for those in her house, for all of them are dressed in red. ²² She makes coverings for herself. Her clothes are linen cloth and purple. ²³ Her husband is known in the gates, when he sits among the leaders of the land. ²⁴ She makes linen clothes and sells them. She brings belts to those who trade. ²⁵ Her clothes are strength and honor. She is full of joy about the future. ²⁶ She opens her mouth with wisdom. The teaching of kindness is on her tongue. ²⁷ She looks well to the ways of those in her house, and does not eat the bread of doing nothing. ²⁸ Her children rise up and honor her. Her husband does also, and he praises her, saying: ²⁹ "Many daughters have done well, but you have done better than all of them." ³⁰ Pleasing ways lie and beauty comes to nothing, but a woman who fears the Lord will be praised. ³¹ Give her the fruit of her hands, and let her works praise her in the gates.

Proverbs 31

LIVING IN GODLY WISDOM

A Journal   **Personal Reflections**

These thoughts are merely my personal meditations as I have reflected on the verses of Proverbs 31 and considered how to apply them to my life. These reflections are not meant to be a commentary or concise textual study. Rather, they are the humble ruminations of my heart.

Proverbs 31:1 (his mother taught him discipline)   *from Lesson 1*

I'm struck by the importance of teaching and influencing others in a positive way. Life is more "caught than taught," but this reminds me to intentionally *make* time to thoughtfully engage with others. We need to encourage self-control, explain healthy relationships, and model godly interactions. How will people know about these things if we don't teach them? The world eagerly displays Satan's lies, and we must share God's truth to develop, protect, and encourage believers.

God talks about training and discipline (a lot) in other verses of Scripture:

- *No discipline seems pleasant at the time, but painful. Later on, however, it produces a harvest of righteousness and peace for those who have been trained by it. Hebrews 12:11*

- *Whoever spares the rod hates their children, but the one who loves their children is careful to discipline them. Proverbs 13:24*

- *Like a city whose walls are broken through is a person who lacks self-control. Proverbs 25:28*

- *For this very reason, make every effort to add to your faith goodness; and to goodness, knowledge; ⁶ and to knowledge, self-control; and to self-*

control, perseverance; and to perseverance, godliness; ^{7} *and to godliness, mutual affection; and to mutual affection, love. 2 Peter 1:5-7*

- *Treat younger men as brothers,* ^{2} *older women as mothers, and younger women as sisters, with absolute purity.* ^{7} *Give the people these instructions, too, so that no one may be open to blame. 1 Timothy 5:1b-2, 7*

Proverbs 31:3 (don't spend your strength on women)   *from Lesson 1*

The paraphrase, "Don't spend your strength on women" really resonates with me. I hear it communicate the empty, uncommitted way that people use each other. Those words echo the self-serving nature of relationships that degrade others and look to use people for their advantage. This is an important warning: don't be the person who treats others this way—and be aware that there *are* people in the world who will treat us like this.

But it also makes me appreciate people who truly invest themselves in others. It makes me thank God for people who *do* make sacrifices for others. They see value, worth, and potential in others and make an investment of love and support. Respect, patience, and sacrifice are given because they see God's bigger plan. Invest in people.

Proverbs 31:8-9 (speak up for the defenseless, defend their rights)   *from Lesson 1*

I am disappointed because I have failed at this in so many ways, and there are so many people who need help. We look past the defenseless and oppressed without even knowing it. God commands us not to just see them but to *act* on their behalf. Speak up and do what you can to help. It would be impossible to list all the places Christians are called to action on behalf of those in need, but there are many ways we can help. Start by praying for an awareness of those in need. Look for opportunities where you can help with your gifts. Set priorities (because we can't do it all) and start working. Encourage others to get involved.

God talks about this in other verses of Scripture:

- *Learn to do right; seek justice.*
  Defend the oppressed.
  Take up the cause of the fatherless;
  plead the case of the widow. Isaiah 1:17

- *You have been a refuge for the poor,*
  a refuge for the needy in their distress,

> *a shelter from the storm*
> *and a shade from the heat. Isaiah 25:4*

- *He has shown you, O mortal, what is good.*
  And what does the Lord require of you?
  To act justly and to love mercy
  and to walk humbly with your God. Micah 6:8

- *Religion that God our Father accepts as pure and faultless is this: to look after orphans and widows in their distress and to keep oneself from being polluted by the world. James 1:27*

This doesn't distract us from the Christ-centered purpose of the church. When we see the needs of the oppressed, we have an opportunity and responsibility to act in Christian love. These actions flow from Christ's love for us, and they continue to spread as we desire to share His love with others. God uses our service for His divine purposes, and He is pleased when we extend His love.

Proverbs 31:10-31 (just a quick note on the entire section)

Proverbs 31:10-31 is an acrostic. Each verse begins with a consecutive letter of the Hebrew alphabet. It isn't as simplistic as our "ABC" song, but it would have aided in memorization and oral teaching. I love these little details that point to God's intricate orderliness.

Proverbs 31:10 (the valuable wife/woman) *from Lesson 2*

This is not simply good marital advice—it's God's familiar announcement that Christian women are a treasure. Scripture has much to say about the value of godly women, and there are several places God speaks to women who are married.

Are you unmarried? Well—only in the earthly sense of the term. Isaiah 54:5-6 says, *"For your Maker is your husband—the Lord Almighty is his name."* You are His wife, and He has given you His image through the gift of the Spirit. Reflect on these verses personally, knowing you are the Bride of Christ:

- *A wife of noble character is her husband's crown. Proverbs 12:4*
  (Consider how your character gives *Him* glory!)

- *He who finds a wife finds what is good and receives favor from the Lord. Proverbs 18:22* (This is God finding you. He doesn't just *find* you, He makes you good!)

Ruth is the only woman in Scripture who is called "noble."

- *All [the] townsmen know that you are a woman of noble character. Ruth 3:11*

Proverbs 31:11 (her husband trusts her)   *from Lesson 2*

I treasure this picture of a trusting, open, and transparent relationship. These are all strong pillars in marriage. Each spouse trusts God to guide, teach, and forgive them individually—then they share those holy gifts with one another. The result is a strong spiritual partnership. This unity sets a firm foundation for godly, selfless leadership and yielding with an undamaged spirit of love.

God talks about trust in other verses of Scripture:

- *Love . . . always trusts. 1 Corinthians 13:7*

- *Those who know your name trust in you, for you, Lord, have never forsaken those who seek you. Psalm 9:10*

- *Trust in the Lord forever, for the Lord, the Lord himself, is the Rock eternal. Isaiah 26:4*

This urges me to build trust in relationships so I can help others understand that God is trustworthy. Trust grows in relationships as we look to the good of others and value their gifts and strengths. The sacrifices we make for people develop trust in relationships. (And when we fail, we know we are forgiven.)

I also love the concept that I can *"safely trust"* my brothers and sisters in Christ. This helps me be honest to give and receive encouragement in times of hardship. Trust builds a healthy partnership that respects and supports spiritual leaders. It also strengthens those who follow leadership because they trust that God will work through the leaders He has appointed.

Finally, *"Her husband . . . lacks nothing of value,"* seems to echo *"The Lord is my shepherd, I lack nothing"* (Psalm 23:1). God faithfully provides everything we need. Just rest in that thought for a minute and see the beautiful description of that relationship! We always see the greatness of God and His perfect love for us. (Thanks for that insight, Pastor Borgwardt!)

Proverbs 31:12 (she does him good, never harm) *from Lesson 2*

This verse raises the standard and expectation for doing good because she brings her husband good "all" the days of her life (not just the days she feels like it or he deserves it). I love the fullness of this concept (once I get over the hammering of the law).

It is interesting to reflect on "all" the days of her life from the perspective of a timeline (not just a daily responsibility). A single woman with a godly reputation will bring respect and honor to the man she marries. People will think more highly of him because she is a wonderful Christian woman (and vice versa). So she is bringing him good before she even marries him. Young women, live in a way that will honor your future husband—and don't forget Christ is your Groom!

But there is another aspect of the timeline we can consider when we talk about "all" her days. Think of the look in a widow's eyes when she lovingly speaks of her husband who has passed away. With kind and loving words, she brings his reputation "*good*" with all her gracious remembrances.

- *The memory of the righteous will be a blessing. Proverbs 10:7*

Proverbs 31:13a (she selects wool and flax) *from Lesson 4*

This makes me think about what I select. This woman knows a lot about textiles and makes careful choices about her wool and weaving. I see a connection between what she learns and what she chooses. This is a good reminder (with lots of applications) that making wise choices sometimes involves a little homework.

Proverbs 31:13b (she works with willing/eager hands) *from Lesson 4*

I know how I should feel when I work—and I often fall short of this command. But we are still commanded to work, even when we aren't willing and eager. I go to work even when I don't feel like it or have a bad attitude (I just try to hide it). I try to focus on my work instead of thinking about other people who should be helping. I try to be kind to people even when my heart feels a million miles away. There are so many ways I fall short of this. I pray that God would strengthen me to fight against my sinful nature and do the right thing with the right attitude.

- *Therefore, my dear friends, as you have always obeyed—not only in my presence, but now much more in my absence—continue to work out your salvation with fear and trembling, [13] for it is God who works in you to will and* *to act in order to fulfill his good purpose. *¹⁴*Do everything without grumbling or arguing,* ¹⁵ *so that you may become blameless and pure, "children of God without fault in a warped and crooked generation." Then you will shine among them like stars in the sky. Philippians 2:12-15*

As I think about learning (verse 13a) and then being eager (verse 13b), I wonder how eager I am to share what I have learned about Scripture. How do I use what God has taught me? Do I remember it is best to start by reading Scripture and let God work the eagerness? Sometimes I rush forward, inspired by my own wisdom, and fall flat on my face. This reminds me to sit quietly, listen, and learn first.

- *The unfolding of your words gives light;*
  it gives understanding to the simple. Psalm 119:130

- *Reflect on what I am saying, for the Lord will give you insight into all this.*
  2 Timothy 2:7

Proverbs 31:14 (she is like a merchant ship)   *from Lesson 5*

I love being a creative *"merchant ship"* that brings blessings to my family. We love to celebrate holidays and birthdays with special meals and traditions. Maybe you host a party with someone's favorite dessert (our family favorite is ice cream cake!). Maybe you buy exquisite chocolate—it feels delightful to make someone happy, especially when it involves food. Sometimes we make food for a family in need, bringing hope and help right to their doorstep. We go places to help and give love. We find creative opportunities like cards, flowers, caroling, yard work, or paying it forward at the drive-thru. It is fun to think about new ways to bless others!

Hospitality is another fantastic opportunity to extend God's love to others right in your own home! Invite friends and neighbors over for coffee, wine, or your new dessert recipe. You can make it fun with exotic food like that of the merchant ship, or have a simple cup of tea. Keep it fun and casual so you aren't stressed out (then you can do it more often).

It's not what's on the table that's important, it's what's on the chairs.

Proverbs 31:15 (she gets up while it's still dark)   *from Lesson 4*

This passage gives us a weighted picture of how God's people approach work and responsibility with effort and commitment. It's a bewildering concept unless we focus on the woman's spirit rather than her schedule. Think about her willingness and purpose more than her alarm clock. We see godly humility and leadership as this woman considers what others need to be successful. Even if she has a lot to do, she takes time to think about what others need. This can be very simple—does your child need to pack a lunch for school? Maybe your child is responsible for that task, but you make sure there is bread and peanut butter. Now think about that on a larger scale (although buying peanut butter *is* one way you do this!). Ask yourself, "What can I do to help others succeed today at home, school, or work?"

Here are some passages to remember—and you might ask yourself, "How can I bring God's love to others in the morning and start their day with joy?"

- *Let the morning bring me word of your unfailing love,*
  for I have put my trust in you. Psalm 143:8

- *Satisfy us in the morning with your unfailing love,*
  that we may sing for joy and be glad all our days. Psalm 90:14

- *Yet this I call to mind*
  and therefore I have hope:
  [22] Because of the LORD's great love we are not consumed,
  for his compassions never fail.
  [23] They are new every morning;
  great is your faithfulness. Lamentations 3:21-23

Proverbs 31:16 (she considers a field and buys it) *from Lesson 5*

The idea of buying a field and planting a vineyard underscores her business and management skills as well as her capability to save and manage her profits. It points to her abilities rather than emphasizing her financial independence. Her business ventures don't pull her heart and love away from others (especially her husband and family). She isn't trying to prove something or make money for herself. But she does make money and deliberately invests her profits. And it makes God look good—it honors Him because she is using her gifts well and wisely.

Scripture also offers this wisdom:

- *Now listen, you who say, "Today or tomorrow we will go to this or that city, spend a year there, carry on business and make money." [14] Why, you do not even know what will happen tomorrow. What is your life? You are a mist that appears for a little while and then vanishes. [15] Instead, you ought to say, "If it is the Lord's will, we will live and do this or that." James 4:13-15*

Let's make a spiritual application with the idea of considering what is wise or best. Researching real estate means looking for solid answers to important questions. Spiritually speaking, we compare and analyze or *"consider"* things by holding them up to the truth of Scripture. We don't just follow someone's recommendation or opinion. We find the truth by searching the Bible—not with human reason but with the promised guidance of the Holy Spirit. The careful and intentional study of His Word will give us wisdom to discern and understand His truth.

- *Dear friends, do not believe every spirit, but test the spirits to see whether they are from God, because many false prophets have gone out into the world. [2] This is how you can recognize the Spirit of God: Every spirit that acknowledges that Jesus Christ has come in the flesh is from God, [3] but every spirit that does not acknowledge Jesus is not from God. 1 John 4:1-3*

- *Do not conform to the pattern of this world, but be transformed by the renewing of your mind. Then you will be able to test and approve what God's will is—his good, pleasing and perfect will. Romans 12:2*

Proverbs 31:17 (she is strong and works vigorously) *from Lesson 4*

I wish strong arms and vigorous work were metaphors. But there is sweat in this verse that runs down her face and drips off her nose. Physical labor is part of working in God's Kingdom. Be thankful when you can work—and remember God gave work for our benefit. Pray for a harvest but keep weeding.

- *The Lord God took the man and put him in the Garden of Eden to work it and take care of it. Genesis 2:15* (There was work *before* there was sin).

- *By the sweat of your brow you will eat your food until you return to the ground. Genesis 3:19* (I wonder if this means sweat came *after* sin!)

- *Obey them not only to win their favor when their eye is on you, but as slaves of Christ, doing the will of God from your heart. Ephesians 6:6*

- *The hardworking farmer should be the first to receive a share of the crops. 2 Timothy 2:6*

- *All hard work brings a profit. Proverbs 14:23* (This is wisdom, not a promise.)

A Journal - Personal Reflections

Proverbs 31:18 (her trading is profitable, her lamp does not go out at night)   *from Lesson 5*

Money is not a Christian's first priority, but we do balance our checkbooks, utilize budgets, and move our investments. There is nothing ungodly about paying attention to those details or being diligent with our resources. It is God-pleasing to learn about wise money management. Good stewardship and financial planning honor God. This woman's skills and abilities in this area are quite evident!

- *Dishonest money dwindles away,*
  but whoever gathers money little by little makes it grow. Proverbs 13:11

Jesus used examples of financial/strategic planning to teach the cost of discipleship.

- *Suppose one of you wants to build a tower. Won't you first sit down and estimate the cost to see if you have enough money to complete it?* [29] *For if you lay the foundation and are not able to finish it, everyone who sees it will ridicule you,* [30] *saying, 'This person began to build and wasn't able to finish.'*
  [31] *"Or suppose a king is about to go to war against another king. Won't he first sit down and consider whether he is able with ten thousand men to oppose the one coming against him with twenty thousand?* [32] *If he is not able, he will send a delegation while the other is still a long way off and will ask for terms of peace. Luke 14:28-32*

I appreciate it when churches do well at keeping their finances open to the congregation yet still find the right balance of not making budgets the focal point. Thanks to the men and women who are behind the scenes serving this way!

Proverbs 31:19 (she holds the distaff and spindle)   *from Lesson 4*

I love the honor and eagerness exhibited by the women of Israel when Moses told the people what was needed for the Tabernacle. God commanded the Israelites to build and furnish a place for worship, and the people willingly responded.

- *Everyone who was willing and whose heart moved them came and brought an offering to the Lord for the work on the tent of meeting, for all its service, and for the sacred garments.* [24] *Everyone who had blue, purple or scarlet yarn or fine linen, or goat hair, ram skins dyed red or the other durable leather brought them.* [25] *Every skilled woman spun with her hands and brought what she had spun—blue, purple or scarlet yarn or fine linen.* [26] *And all the women who were willing and had the skill spun the goat hair. Exodus 35:21, 23, 25-26*

We all have different skills and ways to serve God—but there are many references in Scripture to things that are skillfully woven. With that picture in mind, reflect on this passage and the concept that you are skillfully woven as God's handiwork:

- *For we are God's handiwork, created in Christ Jesus to do good works, which God prepared in advance for us to do. Ephesians 2:10*

Proverbs 31:20 (she opens her arms and extends herself to the needy)   *from Lesson 4*

Paul rejoiced over believers who extended themselves and gave generous gifts though they were poor. Their first love was for God and His church—and the selfless actions of these people demonstrated their gratitude and commitment.

- *And now, brothers and sisters, we want you to know about the grace that God has given the Macedonian churches. ^{2} In the midst of a very severe trial, their overflowing joy and their extreme poverty welled up in rich generosity. ^{3} For I testify that they gave as much as they were able, and even beyond their ability. Entirely on their own, ^{4} they urgently pleaded with us for the privilege of sharing in this service to the Lord's people. ^{5} And they exceeded our expectations: They gave themselves first of all to the Lord, and then by the will of God also to us. 2 Corinthians 8:1-5 (Macedonia is modern day Greece. It is the area where Lydia lived. She is mentioned in Lesson Five.)*

There is also a beautiful Old Testament account of a woman who extended herself to serve God's prophet, Elisha. She wanted to do more than just feed him as he passed by. You can read the story in 2 Kings 4:8-37. This is how it begins:

- *One day Elisha went on to Shunem, where a wealthy woman lived, who urged him to eat some food. So whenever he passed that way, he would turn in there to eat food. ^{9} And she said to her husband, "Behold now, I know that this is a holy man of God who is continually passing our way. ^{10} Let us make a small room on the roof with walls and put there for him a bed, a table, a chair, and a lamp, so that whenever he comes to us, he can go in there." 2 Kings 4:8-10*

Jesus told the parable of the Good Samaritan to show what it looks like to extend yourself to help those in need. You can read the story in Luke 10:25-37.

- *But a Samaritan, as he traveled, came where the man was; and when he saw him, he took pity on him. ^{34} He went to him and bandaged his wounds, pouring on oil and wine. Then he put the man on his own donkey, brought him to an inn and took care of him. ^{35} The next day he took out two denarii and gave them to the innkeeper. "Look after him," he said, "and when I return, I will reimburse you for any extra expense you may have." Luke 10:33-35*

Yet, there is one account of being extended that stands as the greatest sacrifice of all time.

> Upon the cross extended,
>> see, world, your Lord suspended;
>>> your Savior yields his breath.
>
> The Prince of life from heaven
> himself has freely given
>> to shame and blows and bitter death.
>
> I caused your grief and sighing
>> by evils multiplying
>>> as countless as the sands.
>
> I caused the woes unnumbered
> with which your soul is cumbered,
>> your sorrows raised by wicked hands.
>
> Your soul in griefs unbounded,
>> your head with thorns surrounded,
>>> you died to ransom me.
>
> The cross for me enduring,
> the crown for me securing,
>> you healed my wounds and set me free.

Text: Public domain

Proverbs 31:21 (no fear when it snows, her household is clothed) *from Lesson 5*

I envy this perfect balance of recognizing trouble and resting in security. I long for wisdom to live between calm awareness and appropriate action. There is *so much* danger and evil in this world that unsettles me, and I can't pretend I live in a bubble. But God gives me wisdom to make decisions that will keep me safe and protect my loved ones. I do everything I can to stay safe, but I do not live in fear.

A Journal - Personal Reflections

- *[God's] perfect love drives out fear. 1 John 4:18a*

Spiritually, I see application here as parents strive to raise their children in the grace of God. Every parent fails and feels the guilt of not doing enough. But this verse quietly reminds us to do our best as parents and put our confidence in God. Use the gifts He has given to strengthen and clothe your family in the Word—then trust in God's faithfulness and perfect robe of righteousness (even for you as a parent!).

- *Start children off on the way they should go,*
    and even when they are old they will not turn from it. Proverbs 22:6

Proverbs 31:22 (she makes bed-coverings and wears purple linen) *from Lesson 4*

The phrase "purple linen" makes me think of a woman clothed in dignity. It's important to think about how we dress—and why we should care about what we wear. Connect this thought with Proverbs 31:12, that we should bring [men] good, not evil. Don't minimize the responsibility we have to encourage our brothers in faith! If your low-cut outfit fuels sexual attraction, wear it at home for your husband. Help the guys out. Don't stir up the sinful desires they're trying so hard to conquer. Bear God's image as a woman. Live as an example of His perfect design.

The following devotion captures God's desire for how Christian women dress:

Modest Is Hottest by Dawn Schulz

I also want the women to dress modestly, with decency and propriety, adorning themselves, not with elaborate hairstyles or gold or pearls or expensive clothes, but with good deeds, appropriate for women who profess to worship God.
1 Timothy 2:9-10.

You're HOT!

I'm sure you hear those words a lot. Girls are under a great deal of pressure today to be hot. In case you don't know what hot is, let me describe what she looks like. A hot girl is edgy, daring, and thrilling. A hot girl says things like, "People will always talk, so let's give them sumthin to talk about." (Lady Gaga) A hot girl is rebellious. She will always press the limit. Hot girls don't wait for attention to be given to them, they take it. They have sass and attitude. And the most important thing to know about hot girls is that they are always surrounded by hot guys.

Since hot is in, stores do their best to make sure you look the part. They sell clothes that are too tight on the bum and show way too much chest. Advertising tries to convince you that this is the only way to make sure you don't look like your grandma, or worse yet, your mom. Music videos and song lyrics play their part as well. They show you how hot girls dance and tell you what hot girls do with hot guys.

Hot girls also give a very clear message about who they are. And the message is this: I want you to notice ME and I will do whatever it takes to make that happen, even if it's wrong. If my chest causes you to lust, so be it, at least I got your attention. If my short skirt makes you wonder what's underneath, I don't care! At least I've got you thinking. And, girls, what the guy is thinking is "If a hot girl shows this much in public, how much will she show in private?"

God's Word is very clear. It says that what the world calls hot is not appropriate for women who profess to worship God. It says to be modest, decent, and adorned with good deeds. In case you don't know what this looks like, let me describe her. A modest girl is interesting, thoughtful, and humble. She recognizes the gifts she's been given, including her amazing body, but doesn't flaunt them. She knows she could go beyond the limits but chooses to stay within them out of respect for others. She notices, appreciates, and encourages others. Modest girls are graceful and loving. And a modest girl is surrounded by a variety of people because she is genuine in her relationships.

Since a modest girl wants to honor God with her body, she makes the extra effort to select clothing that flatters and enhances her beauty without revealing every detail of it. She covers her breasts because they are special and she is saving them for her husband. A modest girl has respect for modest boys and chooses not to wear the short skirt that might cause him to lust. The filth and immorality found in certain music, movies and pop culture have no part in her life because a modest girl knows they can influence how she acts.

Modest girls do this because they intend to give a very clear message. And the message is this: I don't need to be noticed by you. And I don't want your approval. My heavenly Father sought me out. He sent his son, Jesus, whose perfect life and death have washed me clean. I am set apart and loved by God because of Jesus. That's all the approval I need. Whatever I do, whatever I say, and whatever I wear is not to focus your attention on me. It's to give honor and glory to my God and say thank you to him with everything I have.

Here's the surprising thing: a modest girl is hot. People are drawn to her. In fact, at some point a modest girl will probably be told, "You're hot!" She shouldn't feel bad about that. Some people don't have the right words. Instead she'll treat this as she does every other form of earthly praise. She'll offer it up in thanks to God. He made her. He loves her. And he saved her, giving her everything she has. A modest girl simply wants to live her life in a way that is appropriate for one who professes to worship him.

Proverbs 31:23 (her husband is respected at the city gates) *from Lesson 3*

The picture of this respected man at the city gates inspires me to appreciate his leadership and strength. Consider his witness and influence, then think about Jesus' words:

- *"You are the light of the world. A town built on a hill cannot be hidden. [15] Neither do people light a lamp and put it under a bowl. Instead they put it on its stand, and it gives light to everyone in the house. [16] In the same way, let your light shine before others, that they may see your good deeds and glorify your Father in heaven." Matthew 4:14-16*

I like to think of the godly man at the city gate like a city on a hill. You can't miss him as he offers security and protection to others. He is strong, reliable, and wise. He is not afraid of the darkness but stands with undiminished light. Thank God for the people in your life who stand as a strong influence and witness for Christ. They are a great blessing. Support and appreciate them. Follow their example.

Proverbs 31:24 (she makes and sells garments) *from Lesson 5*

This is 1000 B.C. Etsy. It captures the idea of a creative entrepreneur who takes a skill or idea and brings it to completion. If you've ever done anything like this, you know how incredibly hard it is—congrats to you! Most of us have a lot of unfinished projects stuffed in a closet.

Proverbs 31:25a (she is clothed with strength and dignity) *from Lesson 3*

The words "strength" and "dignity" echo the description in Proverbs 31:10 that this woman is strong and noble. But her strength is not a fiery self-sufficiency, and her dignity is not pretentious. God's faithfulness is her strength, and her dignity flows from a life guided by the wisdom of Scripture.

We stumble foolishly when we clutch our own strength and stand stubbornly with prideful determination. That isn't true strength. True strength comes from God when we are emptied of ourselves and filled with Christ.

- *But he said to me, "My grace is sufficient for you, for my power is made perfect in weakness." Therefore I will boast all the more gladly about my weaknesses, so that Christ's power may rest on me. ¹⁰ That is why, for Christ's sake, I delight in weaknesses, in insults, in hardships, in persecutions, in difficulties. For when I am weak, then I am strong. 2 Corinthians 12:9-10*

Other times we are weak with fear or worry. Hopelessness can overwhelm us, and we feel anything but strong—yet God faithfully comes to our aid.

- *He gives strength to the weary
  and increases the power of the weak. Isaiah 40:29*

- *So do not fear, for I am with you; do not be dismayed, for I am your God. I will strengthen you and help you; I will uphold you with my righteous right hand. Isaiah 41:10*

- *But the Lord is faithful, and he will strengthen you and protect you from the evil one. 2 Thessalonians 3:3*

Proverbs 31:25b (she can laugh at the days to come) *from Lesson 3*

There is no assurance that our days will be filled with laughter from an earthly perspective. Our confidence in the future comes from God's promise to work in and through us. This is not an easy life with earthly victories. It is optimistic joy that trusts God's plan. We know He is working out His good and perfect plans in us.

- *In all things God works for the good of those who love him, who have been called according to his purpose. ²⁹ For those God foreknew he also predestined to be conformed to the image of his Son, that he might be the firstborn among many brothers and sisters. Romans 8:28-29*

But in this world, we are filled with joyful delight because we are free from the guilt of sin and death—it no longer rules and enslaves us! We are blessed with the comfort of the Holy Spirit (John 14:16-17, 26), a loving Savior who redeemed us (1 Peter 1:18-19), and peace with God (Ephesians 2:14-16). With these blessings, we have a joyful spirit because we are free in Christ!

- *For God did not give us a spirit of timidity, but a spirit of power, of love and of self-discipline. 2 Timothy 1:7*

- *But as for me, I am filled with power, with the Spirit of the Lord, and with justice and might. Micah 3:8*

A Journal - Personal Reflections

Proverbs 31:26 (she speaks with wisdom and faithful instruction)   *from Lesson 3*

Godly wisdom comes only from being in His Word. It starts as each one of us spends time in Scripture, reading, studying, and listening to God.

- *The fear of the Lord is the beginning of wisdom. Proverbs 9:10*

- *For the Lord gives wisdom;*
  from his mouth come knowledge and understanding. Proverbs 2:6

Don't think of godly wisdom in a casual way, as if it were just good advice. The words of wisdom we speak reflect the truth of Scripture, and they are spoken with a desire to help others understand. Our words should benefit others.

- *You, however, must teach what is appropriate to sound doctrine. ³ Teach the older women to . . . teach what is good. Titus 2:1, 3*

- *[Speak] the truth in love. Ephesians 4:15*

- *Do not let any unwholesome talk come out of your mouths, but only what is helpful for building others up according to their needs, that it may benefit those who listen. Ephesians 4:29*

This begins in our homes.

- *These commandments that I give you today are to be on your hearts. ⁷ Impress them on your children. Talk about them when you sit at home and when you walk along the road, when you lie down and when you get up. ⁸ Tie them as symbols on your hands and bind them on your foreheads. ⁹ Write them on the doorframes of your houses and on your gates. Deuteronomy 6:6-9*

The love and importance of Christian homes is repeated throughout Scripture. In a society that is confused and decaying, our call to live as Christian men, women, and families is urgent. The witness of Christian families, loving marriages, and valued children is desperately needed to help people see and learn about God's good design for humanity. We are surrounded by people who don't really know who they are or how they can find peace. Christian homes can extend God's love and peace as they model His grace, forgiveness, and love. Your home won't be perfect, but God commands us to teach Scripture to our families and let our light shine. God wants to strengthen your family with His Word and gives you the opportunity to show others grace in action.

I also love the way God gave His people ceremonies and festivals to remind them of His promises and faithfulness. Today, parents take special time on a child's birthday to retell their birth story, remember the faith planted in their heart at baptism, and recount the many blessings of God. In our family, we have a tradition of reading Luke 2 on Christmas Eve before we open presents to remember the gift of our Savior. At Easter, we announce, "Christos Anesti" (Christ is Risen) when we crack our Easter eggs to celebrate the empty tomb. Be creative (like the merchant ship!) as you seek ways or traditions to share God's Word in your home.

- *"When you enter the land that the Lord will give you as he promised, observe this ceremony. ^{26} And when your children ask you, 'What does this ceremony mean to you?' ^{27} then tell them, 'It is the Passover sacrifice to the Lord, who passed over the houses of the Israelites in Egypt and spared our homes when he struck down the Egyptians.'" Then the people bowed down and worshiped. Exodus 12:25-27*

Another aspect of faithful teaching is the daily, ordinary opportunity we have in relationships to speak influential words of truth. Not just the "big" events in life or long, intense conversations. Small nuggets of wisdom are a blessing.

- *Be wise in the way you act toward outsiders; make the most of every opportunity. Let your conversation be always full of grace, seasoned with salt, so that you may know how to answer everyone. Colossians 4:5-6*

- *A word spoken at the right time
     is like golden apples in silver settings.
  ^{12} To ears that listen, a wise person's correction is like a gold ring
     or like jewelry made of pure gold. Proverbs 25:11-12 EHV*

- *The lips of the righteous nourish many. Proverbs 10:21*

Proverbs 31:27 (she watches over household affairs) *from Lesson 5*

Godly wisdom includes management of household affairs.

- *Good food and olive oil are stored up in the dwellings of the wise,
  but a foolish person devours everything he has. Proverbs 21:20*

- *The plans of the diligent lead to profit
     as surely as haste leads to poverty. Proverbs 21:5*

- *So if you have not been trustworthy in handling worldly wealth, who will trust you with true riches? Luke 16:11*

This watchfulness suggests good stewardship and orderliness, but more importantly, there is an aura of peace in her home. She oversees a haven of rest, not an immaculate mansion. Her home is open to ministry opportunities and outreach; it is a place where grace richly flows. In our lives, neighbors, friends, and children enter our doors and we have opportunities to share Christ. Those people don't need a perfectly clean house—they need the peace and grace of Jesus.

The wife's participation in the management of the household gives us a glimpse of how healthy marriages and godly partnerships work. There is trust and teamwork as each person serves the common good with harmony and respect. The tone of the verse makes it noticeably clear that there is leadership in their home, and she is not hedging against her husband's leadership—she is honoring it. The entire chapter has described a loving husband who is the head of the home and accountable to God. The wife's active participation and gifts are a visible witness to her husband's loving leadership and a living example of how women use their gifts in partnership and under headship—fully engaged, remarkably skilled, and selflessly respectful. God is showing us something He wants us to see. And it is good.

Proverbs 31:28 (her children and husband praise her) *from Lesson 3*

What a joy to hear the family give her praise! You *want* her to receive acclamations and know that she is appreciated. Follow this example and express your delight and thanksgiving for the people around you. Be the person who gives thanks for the service of others. Look for them and extend yourself to say thank you.

Celebrate when others succeed. This might be an accomplishment at school or work. It may be finishing chemo or running a marathon. Rejoice and be happy in their success—praise their efforts. Let any hints of jealousy be crushed by the confidence that God gives good gifts and grants success to each of His children.

- *All these are the work of one and the same Spirit, and he gives them to each one, just as he determines. [18] But in fact God has arranged the parts in the body, every one of them, just as he wanted them to be. 1 Corinthians 12:11, 18*

- *Rejoice with those who rejoice. Romans 12:15*

Proverbs 31:29 (the words of praise from her husband) *from Lesson 2*

There is something special about words of praise from your husband but this is a wonderful place to remember that the Lord is your husband. Think of His words (and *deeds*) of encouragement, praise, and love for you!

- *The Lord your God is with you. . . . He takes great delight in you. He will quiet you with his love. He will rejoice over you with singing. Zephaniah 3:17 EHV*

- *You will be a crown of splendor in the Lord's hand,*
  a royal diadem in the hand of your God.
  ⁴ . . . the Lord will take delight in you,
  and [you] will be married.
  ⁵ . . . as a bridegroom rejoices over his bride,
  so will your God rejoice over you. Isaiah 62:3-5
- *For God so loved the world that he gave his one and only Son, that whoever believes in him shall not perish but have eternal life. John 3:16*

These words also apply to the Bride of Christ. Words of praise from other believers are especially important. Speak kindly with thanksgiving to build unity in the body of Christ. Rejoice when others are honored.

- *If one part [of the body] is honored, every part rejoices with it. 1 Corinthians 12:26*

Proverbs 31:30a (charm is deceitful, beauty is fading) *from Lesson 2*

The first phrase of this verse about charm and beauty can easily be overlooked because the last half of the verse (about faith) is so important. But these first words point to sins we must not overlook. Sometimes, women pursue the attention of men by flaunting cheap charm and outward beauty. Sexual attention can be flattering and exhilarating—it can seem thrilling and powerful. But Scripture confirms what we know in our hearts and perhaps have experienced—such pursuits lead to emptiness and pain. Sin erodes faith and separates us from God. A woman may enjoy stirring the desires of men, but she is playing with fire that can rage out of control with a wide path of destruction.

How do we protect young women from these dangers? How do we warn them against temptations to misuse charm, beauty, and the power of sexuality? We talk about it and show them Scripture's warnings. We build safe, secure relationships where we can discuss important, personal things and allow young women to ask questions. We demonstrate loving encouragement and concern for others. We take time to give them attention and make ourselves available to listen. This is *such* a different attitude than feeling we are obligated to warn young women with a tone of disgust as if we never face such temptations. We all face temptation, and all our sins are an offense to God (remember Lesson One?).

Proverbs 31:30b (a woman who fears the Lord is to be praised)   *from Lesson 2*

Here is the heart of the matter. This woman is a redeemed child of God.

Every page of this scrapbook has been crafted under the theme of God's grace.

I have friends who are true scrapbook fanatics, and they are very deliberate and intentional in their themes and planning. As God planned and crafted all of these beautiful pages to teach us about relationships, service, and leadership, we know they would be empty and meaningless without faith in God. With the richness of grace, every page of our life is beautiful and filled with His holy purpose.

- *And without faith it is impossible to please God, because anyone who comes to him must believe that he exists and that he rewards those who earnestly seek him. Hebrews 11:6*

- *Your beauty should not come from outward adornment, such as elaborate hairstyles and the wearing of gold jewelry or fine clothes. [4] Rather, it should be that of your inner self, the unfading beauty of a gentle and quiet spirit, which is of great worth in God's sight. 1 Peter 3:3-4*

Proverbs 31:31 (give her a reward and praise)   *from Lesson 3*

God says this woman should receive thanks and praise at the city gate—a public place where leaders conduct business. She has served with grace, love, and selfless humility—and Scripture says the leaders should thank her. The men at the city gate express praise and appreciation for her gifts and service—and God is pleased.

This is a powerful verdict against those who accuse Scripture of revering men more than women. It leaves no room for questions about a woman's value or worth in God's eyes. The scene of the Proverbs woman at the gate gives us a flashback to the Garden of Eden, where God gives equal value and godly partnership. Like the men at the gate, Adam is pleased and thankful for Eve. But just as God established order at creation, in Proverbs 31, God mentions the city gate. He honors the place and position of leadership given to men. He shows how men in leadership should treat women. He shows His perfect design as we see the men express their appreciation and praise for the woman. The design is equal and orderly.

Proverbs 31 teaches men how to be Christ-like as they love women. This chapter has displayed the life of a godly woman and the actions of men who love her in a way that honors God. Women don't shake this passage in the face of godly men. We live in it. We see the love and appreciation in the body of Christ. We pursue holy relationships and partnerships that imitate God's beautiful description. We delight in the blessings of God's design—they are rich and magnificent. Thank you Jesus! And thank you to the men who do a wonderful job of living in God's design.

Perhaps we should also look at this passage from another perspective and consider how we might be positioned at a city gate to *give* a reward or praise. Has God put you in a place where you can give good things or kindness to others? If you look, it isn't hard to see how you can bless those around you. Even if you're not a leader at the city gate, you can thank the people around you. Take time to notice the service of others and express your appreciation—especially if it is in your power to act with a reward and praise.

- *Do not withhold good from those to whom it is due, when it is in your power to act. Proverbs 3:27*

Finally, meditate on this verse to remember the Savior who has won your salvation and stands at the gates of heaven to give you the reward of His victory! Hear His words of praise and joy:

- *Well done, good and faithful servant! Matthew 25:23*

The humbling insight here is that Christ speaks these words of praise. He is the one who gives the reward. Even more, He is the one who paid the full price for that reward with His life and death. It is His Spirit who bears the fruit of good deeds in our lives. He enables us to do the works He has prepared for us. It is all God's work, done with the gifts He has given us.

May the name of Jesus be praised.

A Journal - Personal Reflections

This chart may help you personally apply the wisdom of Proverbs 31.

Proverbs 31 Applications and Attitudes

Am I eager and willing, motivated by the Gospel? Am I kind, thoughtful, and generous as I look to serve my family and others?	She opens her arms to the poor and extends her hands to the needy.
	She makes coverings for her bed.
	In her hand she holds the distaff and grasps the spindle with her fingers.
	She selects wool and flax and works with eager hands.
Am I creative and open to the opportunities and gifts that God has given me at this time? Are my motives and goals God-pleasing?	She considers a field and buys it; out of her earnings she plants a vineyard.
	She makes linen garments and sells them, and supplies the merchants with sashes.
	She is like the merchant ships, bringing her food from afar.
Am I doing my best and trusting God for the outcome? Am I a hard worker who manages my time and gifts well?	She sees that her trading is profitable, and her lamp does not go out at night.
	She sets about her work vigorously; her arms are strong for her tasks.
	She watches over the affairs of her household and does not eat the bread of idleness.
Am I a servant leader, concerned about those around me?	She gets up while it is still dark; she provides food for her family and portions for her servant girls.
Am I free of guilt when I do things for myself?	She is clothed in fine linen and purple.

Answer Helps Lesson One: Meet the Woman – Her Introduction

1. In a chapter that portrays the beauty and value of Christian women, why do the opening verses have a masculine tone?

   This mother is guiding and teaching her son—she uses examples and warnings that would be specific to him as a man and a king. She wants him to be a good husband and wise leader. Think of how a mother's advice to her son is different than a father's advice.

2. What influences and examples today heighten the importance of sharing this godly advice and encouragement with young men and women?

   The world still lacks good examples, and society makes sinful lifestyles look normalized and appealing. If we don't teach and train children in the ways of the Lord, the world will gladly and easily take up the task of teaching them the opposite. God calls parents (and believers) to teach and encourage children in faith and godly living.

3. Where can you offer godly wisdom like Lemuel's mother, and where could you be more intentional as a Christian influence?

   Women are influential in their homes, extended family, friendships, church, work, and community. Be intentional and outspoken with words of kindness and grace. Take the initiative to make a positive comment and offer encouragement.

4. Identify verses in the book of Esther that highlight her difficult situation.

   The rulers had likely gathered to plan a conquest of the Greeks (Es. 1:3) and "destroy/ruin kings" (Pr. 31:3). Xerxes held a banquet where wine was abundant (Es. 1:7-8), and their excessive drinking fits the warning against kings drinking (Pr. 31:4). Xerxes' command (Es. 1:10-11) would have caused men to lust after Vashti as she paraded in front of them. King Xerxes was a man of rage (Es. 2:1). Haman was selfish, prideful, and longed to oppress the Jews (3:5-6), but Proverbs 31:5 warns against unjust judgments and oppression. Esther spoke up for the Jews (Es. 7:3-4) as God commands in Proverbs 31:8-9.

5. How do the accounts of Esther and Abigail help when your life in Christ is hard, dark, frightening, or traumatic?

   Scripture points to the faithfulness and mercy of God. It tells of His power, control over history, and how He works things for the good of His children. These accounts are written to give us hope and show us the greatness of God so we are not afraid. They teach us to trust God when things seem out of control. They also move us to act, trusting in God at all times.

6. How does the harsh truth about sin prepare and equip you to learn about living as a godly woman?

   It reminds me how desperately I need a Savior and that I will never measure up. I know I can't do it on my own. Refreshed with the Gospel, the law guides me in holy living. This world will never be without sin (my own or that of others). Even when I fail, I am forgiven.

7. How does the loving truth about Christ's completed work of redemption prepare and equip you to learn about living as a godly woman?

   It is done! I am free to serve with no required expectation or standard. I don't have to do anything to earn His favor. My responses of love are merely an expression of gratefulness for grace. I can honor Him, and He is pleased when I serve Him from a heart of faith.

Answer Helps Lesson 2: Look in the Mirror – Her Image

1. Describe ways you have seen glimpses of God's image in other godly women.

    God's image is evident in women's compassion, Biblical insights, desire for the things of God, wisdom, or concern to resist things that are evil. We see Him through a woman's love for family, church, and people. Women reflect God as they show a commitment to things that are important to God and a willingness to help. Their witness also includes general qualities that reflect God, such as gentleness, kindness, patience, or other fruits of the Spirit.

2. What can women do to encourage one another to live as a new creation in Christ?

    Include God's Word and wisdom in your conversations. Listen, love, pray, and most of all, point them to the Word! Offer positive godly comments. Speak words that are nurturing.

3. What will change the most as your self-image is realigned with the image of God that has been given to you?

    Answers will vary. For me, it will be my thinking. Scripture gives me truth that equips me to fight Satan's lies. I know my value and worth are not based on how I feel about myself. I don't have worry about being accepted. I am designed, chosen, and redeemed by God. I have His image because He says so, not because I do the right things. I'm forgiven and loved.

4. Compare these verses from Proverbs with Genesis chapters 1-2 and note where you see the similarities.

    Adam's amazement expresses our awe of how God values women (compare Gen. 2:23 and Prov. 31:10). Imagine how Eve felt when she heard God's plan for her to be fruitful and multiply (Gen. 1:28)—it likely felt like the laughter and confidence described in Proverbs 31:25. In Gen. 1:31, at the end of day six, God says His creation is "very good" and His delight is echoed in Proverbs 31:30-31 as He says this woman deserves to be praised.

5. God reveals Himself as a helper, *"Indeed, God is my helper"* (Psalm 54:4, EHV). Since we bear His image, we will also be helpers. Review the life and actions of Mary Magdalene. How does her life reflect and give evidence of the truth that God is a helper?

    At times, Mary traveled with Jesus and the disciples—she would have served them in many ways. Meditate on the thought of Mary standing near the cross with Jesus' mother as He was crucified. A helper extends the love of God to others, and Mary showed that love to Jesus' mother and to Jesus as she stood in reverent trust, love, and friendship while he suffered. She went to the tomb to take care of His body and was greeted by the risen Lord!

6. How do godly men demonstrate that they value godly women?

    Answers will vary: Men appreciate and support women's gifts and strengths with words of thanks and encouragement. Men make sacrifices to help women use their gifts.

7. How does your view of ungodly women help or hinder your outreach?

    In outreach, we remember that unbelievers are slaves to sin. The depravity and ugliness of sin are an urgent reminder of how much people need forgiveness. If we are angry or disgusted by sin, our compassion and love for the lost could be hindered. Hostility can blind us to the spiritual emptiness of others as they seek love and acceptance. Pray for wisdom to follow Christ's example of speaking truth/correction or giving compassion and hope.

Answer Helps Lesson 2: verses to study Mary Magdalene

Matthew 27:55-56, 59-61, 28:1 - *Many women were there, watching from a distance. They had followed Jesus from Galilee to care for his needs. ⁵⁶ Among them were Mary Magdalene, Mary the mother of James and Joseph, and the mother of Zebedee's sons. ⁵⁹ Joseph took the body, wrapped it in a clean linen cloth, ⁶⁰ and placed it in his own new tomb that he had cut out of the rock. He rolled a big stone in front of the entrance to the tomb and went away. ⁶¹ Mary Magdalene and the other Mary were sitting there opposite the tomb.¹ After the Sabbath, at dawn on the first day of the week, Mary Magdalene and the other Mary went to look at the tomb.*

Mark 15:40-41, 47, 16:1-11 - *Some women were watching from a distance. Among them were Mary Magdalene, Mary the mother of James the younger and of Joseph,[d] and Salome. ⁴¹ In Galilee these women had followed him and cared for his needs. Many other women who had come up with him to Jerusalem were also there.*
⁴⁷ Mary Magdalene and Mary the mother of Joseph saw where he was laid.
¹ When the Sabbath was over, Mary Magdalene, Mary the mother of James, and Salome bought spices so that they might go to anoint Jesus' body. ² Very early on the first day of the week, just after sunrise, they were on their way to the tomb ³ and they asked each other, "Who will roll the stone away from the entrance of the tomb?" ⁴ But when they looked up, they saw that the stone, which was very large, had been rolled away. ⁵ As they entered the tomb, they saw a young man dressed in a white robe sitting on the right side, and they were alarmed. ⁶ Don't be alarmed," he said. "You are looking for Jesus the Nazarene, who was crucified. He has risen! He is not here. See the place where they laid him. ⁷ But go, tell his disciples and Peter, 'He is going ahead of you into Galilee. There you will see him, just as he told you.'" ⁸ Trembling and bewildered, the women went out and fled from the tomb. They said nothing to anyone, because they were afraid. ⁹ When Jesus rose early on the first day of the week, he appeared first to Mary Magdalene, out of whom he had driven seven demons. ¹⁰ She went and told those who had been with him and who were mourning and weeping. ¹¹ When they heard that Jesus was alive and that she had seen him, they did not believe it.

Luke 8:1-3, 24:1-11 - *After this, Jesus traveled about from one town and village to another, proclaiming the good news of the kingdom of God. The Twelve were with him, ² and also some women who had been cured of evil spirits and diseases: Mary (called Magdalene) from whom seven demons had come out; ³ Joanna the wife of Chuza, the manager of Herod's household; Susanna; and many others. These women were helping to support them out of their own means.*
¹ On the first day of the week, very early in the morning, the women took the spices they had prepared and went to the tomb. ² They found the stone rolled away from the tomb, ³ but when they entered, they did not find the body of the Lord Jesus. ⁴ While they were wondering about this, suddenly two men in clothes that gleamed like lightning stood beside them. ⁵ In their fright the women bowed down with their faces to the ground, but the men said to them, "Why do you look for the living among the dead? ⁶ He is not here; he has risen! Remember how he told you, while he was still with you in Galilee: ⁷ 'The Son of Man must be delivered over to the hands of sinners, be crucified and on the third day be raised again.' " ⁸ Then they remembered his words. ⁹ When they came back from the tomb, they told all these things to the Eleven and to all the others. ¹⁰ It was Mary Magdalene, Joanna, Mary the mother of James, and the others with them who told this to the apostles. ¹¹ But they did not believe the women, because their words seemed to them like nonsense.

John 19:25, 20:1-2, 11-18 - *Near the cross of Jesus stood his mother, his mother's sister, Mary the wife of Clopas, and Mary Magdalene. ¹ Early on the first day of the week, while it was still dark, Mary Magdalene went to the tomb and saw that the stone had been removed from the entrance. ² So she came running to Simon Peter and the other disciple, the one Jesus loved, and said, "They have taken the Lord out of the tomb, and we don't know where they have put him!" ¹¹ Now Mary stood outside the tomb crying. As she wept, she bent over to look into the tomb ¹² and saw two angels in white, seated where Jesus' body had been, one at the head and the other at the foot. ¹³ They asked her, "Woman, why are you crying?" "They have taken my Lord away," she said, "and I don't know where they have put him." ¹⁴ At this, she turned around and saw Jesus standing there, but she did not realize that it was Jesus. ¹⁵ He asked her, "Woman, why are you crying? Who is it you are looking for?" Thinking he was the gardener, she said, "Sir, if you have carried him away, tell me where you have put him, and I will get him." ¹⁶ Jesus said to her, "Mary. "She turned toward him and cried out in Aramaic, "Rabboni!" (which means "Teacher"). ¹⁷ Jesus said, "Do not hold on to me, for I have not yet ascended to the Father. Go instead to my brothers and tell them, 'I am ascending to my Father and your Father, to my God and your God.'" ¹⁸ Mary Magdalene went to the disciples with the news: "I have seen the Lord!" And she told them that he had said these things to her.*

Answer Helps Lesson 3: Delight in Her Love – Her Relationships

1. What advice would you give a young woman who is seeking to live in loving, Christ-centered relationships?

    Answers will vary. Encourage women to see others through the eyes of Christ and be guided by God's Word in their actions and conversations. Understand that God's purpose for relationships might be different than ours. Forgiveness, grace, and fruits of the Spirit will mark relationships. Don't be surprised when <u>you</u> are the one who is blessed!

2. Describe actions that build trust and demonstrate commitment when struggling in a friendship.

    Take the words and actions of others in the kindest possible way. Have respect for words spoken in confidence, put the best construction on everything. Focus on common spiritual goals and make every effort to pursue love and unity. See others with the eyes of Christ.

3. List three people outside your immediate family who might be influenced by you.

    Answers will vary. Think of people at work, church, or in the community. This could be as simple as a bank teller or soccer coach—someone you can befriend.

4. Is there a place outside your comfort zone that God would like you to love others?

    We work to cross both generational and cultural boundaries with God's love, but we should also look nearby to see who we can love. Lesson One reminded us to look for the oppressed or helpless and respond with acts of love. Is there someone you don't want to love—someone awkward whom you hope to avoid, like a neighbor or relative? (Naomi probably felt weird as she started building relationships with Moabite women.)

5. Compare the verses in this lesson to what you know about Mary's life and notice what similarities you find.

    Imagine Joseph's trust in Mary (an angel confirming God's plan would plant some serious trust!). He must have marveled in joy with his hand on her belly, feeling the Savior move in her womb. She did greatly enrich his life! Jesus would have appreciated Mary and expressed His thanks (perfectly). Mary would've gained great wisdom and spiritual insights as Jesus grew up in their home—and would've had many opportunities to share what she learned.

6. Think of someone who has influenced you, describe their impact, and determine how you can follow their example.

    Answers will vary.

7. How can you model the relationships of the Proverbs 31 woman in your community (outside your home and church)?

    Start by recognizing that God has designed and placed you here to be an influence everywhere you go. Develop relationships with neighbors and coworkers, postal workers, and grocery clerks (this list is endless). Show kindness and offer encouragement, especially to the people you see often (but one-time random kindness is good too!). Learn about what is important to them, listen for ways you can help them, and remember them in your prayers. Ask God to show you how you can offer them hope and talk about the forgiveness of Christ. Like the Proverbs 31 woman, offer words of wisdom and kindness.

Answer Helps Lesson 4: Watch Her Serve – Her Tasks

1. Discuss the abilities and interests God has given you. Where have you had the opportunity to use or develop your natural gifts and skills?

   Answers will vary but encourage women to identify what they enjoy doing. Discuss how those gifts or abilities can be a blessing to others (in and out of the church). Look for opportunities to encourage women to value or develop their gifts and skills.

2. What wisdom can you glean from Jesus' words, *"Whatever you did for one of the least of these brothers and sisters of mine, you did for me"* (Matthew 25:40)?

   The Proverbs 31 woman serves others whom many would call "the least of these." Whether servant girls, the poor, or the needy, she is committed to helping others. Her actions demonstrate God's love and equal value of all people. Lesson One showed God's command to help those in need—this lesson allows us to see it happen.

3. When God sees all your work (and the attitude in your heart), does it make you feel guilty or delighted?

   You might feel guilty because you know He sees your failures or sinful motives (UGH). But you might also be delighted because He sees and treasures all your acts of faith that others may not see or appreciate (YAY). It is probably a little of both!

4. What attitudes do you struggle with when you face hard work—and does the expectation of a reward or success ever creep into your thinking?

   We struggle with unwillingness, self-pity, weariness, lack of motivation, resentment toward others who should or could help, irritation, and frustration that labor is not always fruitful.

   And oh, that dreadful, sinful flesh ruins everything! We may even start with good motives, but Satan often throws in selfish expectations that we deserve something for our hard work.

5. Think of the women in your church who serve others. How can you affirm their service and works of faith?

   Verbally and tangibly express your appreciation with thank you notes, happy sticky-notes, flowers, chocolate, or gift cards! Don't feel compelled to offer correction or criticism. Do offer help and support. Tell people about the loving service of others!

6. How does this lesson equip you for times that you can't see the impact of your service?

   We can lose hope or the desire to serve when it feels like our service doesn't make a difference. Hear the truth in this lesson that all our tasks can bring God glory and honor. He chose you to be His servant and do His work. That is your joy and motivation.

7. How can you help those around you see the godly purpose and value of their service or work?

   Say something positive! Mention the work or service of others in a supportive way and talk about how God blesses our labor. God loves it when our hearts are moved to action because of His faithful grace.

Answer Helps Lesson 5: Follow Her Lead – Her Opportunities

1. This woman is affirmed by her husband in Proverbs 31:11, 23, 28. How do you think he supports his wife's leadership opportunities?

    A godly husband offers encouragement and wisdom; he speaks kindly and honestly with insights about his wife that help her. A loving husband makes sacrifices for his wife's good and works things for her benefit. His help at home is a great blessing. Their marriage and partnership include a commitment to help each other and work toward common goals.

2. Based on what you've learned about this woman's character, what do you think her leadership would be like?

    It certainly seems to reflect the leadership of Christ—there is humility, a willingness to sacrifice for the good of others, and a servant heart. We don't see pride, selfishness, or wrong motives. Her leadership would also reflect well on her husband—people would have respect for her husband because of the way she leads.(

3. Discuss the frustrations you've experienced when your leadership doesn't seem successful.

    It can be frustrating when you try to be Christ-like in your leadership and it doesn't seem to work very well. Proverbs 31 only shows us the positive side of her life and leadership, but we know there will be hardships. Scripture also gives us an eternal perspective of how leadership is meant to benefit others. We see God working in and through leaders to accomplish His will. When frustration comes, we still trust God and simply do our best to be faithful, remembering that He is always faithful to us. He has entrusted us with the gift and position of leadership.

4. What important or unique actions did you note in Deborah's life?

    She is respectful and supportive even when Barak struggles. She wants Barak to succeed and follow God's calling. She's not jealous of his position but works to see him win (not the "move-over-I'll-do-it" attitude). She wants God's will and follows God's plan. She doesn't become irritated or arrogant with him when he hesitates and needs encouragement.

5. How do the similarities between Deborah, Lydia, and the Proverbs 31 woman give you encouragement?

    Answers will vary but they are all women who respond to God's love with a desire to serve. They eagerly look for ways to serve that will bless others. They recognize their gifts and skills, and with eyes of faith, they seek and find ways to glorify God in their lives.

6. What key qualities are important in Christian leaders?

    Humility, integrity, honesty, respect, willingness to learn from or admit failure, desire to see others succeed, strength, wisdom, love—all good things that flow from faith.

7. How do you stay focused on the highest calling—that of faith?

    Stay connected to your call to faith through the Word and sacraments. Our actions or obedience will not make us strong. We remember that the devil, the world, and our flesh will be subtle, manipulative, and eager to draw us away from Christ.